# REBUILDING:

## Prayer Lessons from Nehemiah

## By Terry Magee

Rebuilding: Prayer Lessons from the Life of Nehemiah

ISBN: 978-1-7978-6885-1

First Edition: April, 2019

Cover design by Emily Magee

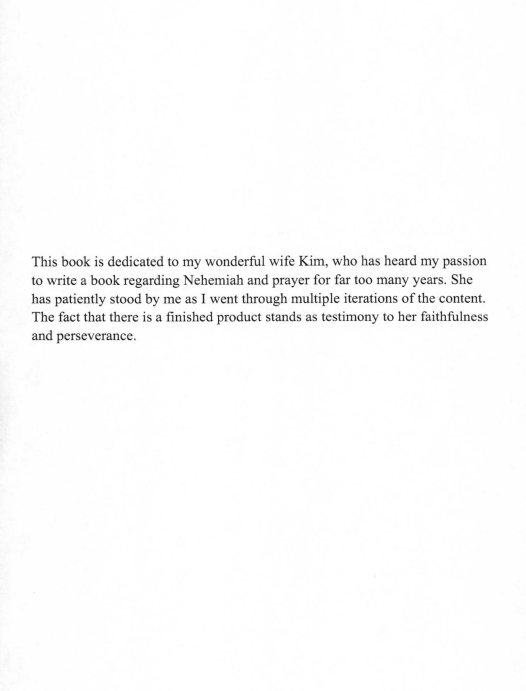

This book is dedicated to my wonderful wife Kim, who has heard my passion to write a book regarding Nehemiah and prayer for far too many years. She has patiently stood by me as I went through multiple iterations of the content. The fact that there is a finished product stands as testimony to her faithfulness and perseverance.

# Table of Contents

# Foreword

Too often we get caught up in the chaos of day to day life and forget the fact that we are to be investing in the future.

How many of you have been blessed to have prayer warriors influence your life--those dear, faithful people who do battle for you specifically behind the scenes because they feel strongly called to do so? I can think of quite a few in my own life: my grandparents, my parents, and my friend Amy, to name a few. They are spiritual pillars in my world, and they seem to have an incredibly special relationship with the Lord through prayer. I know that the Lord has worked mightily through their prayers on my behalf.

Maybe you have a mystical view of prayer and think you need to chant some magic words to have your prayer heard by God or mean something in the great cosmic void. Or, you think prayer involves calling down fire and using words like "smite" and "bequeath."

Or perhaps you have had a disappointing relationship with God through prayer. You don't have a special closet in your house. You don't have spiritual role models who pray for you. You don't have the hours upon hours each day to devote to prayer like the early church seemed to have, and even if you did, you wouldn't know where to start. You may even think the idea of prayer is boring. Maybe you've prayed for something before and haven't received the response you hoped for.

*What if I told you instead that there was a simple way to incorporate prayer into your everyday life?* A way for you set aside your preconceived notions of prayer and allow God to truly transform your life? That ultimately the discipline of prayer was not about you?

In *Rebuilding: Prayer Lessons from the Life of Nehemiah*, Terry takes you step by step through the recorded life of one of the Bible's lesser known characters--Nehemiah--and shows you how to build your prayer life. So often we say "all we can do now is pray" when faced with challenges, but Terry shows us how to truly live a life of prayer and delight in God's presence at all times. Prayer is not just for the super spiritual people. It's not just for the people in movies. It's not a mystical sense or magical incantation. Sometimes God doesn't answer prayers the way we want Him to. And, if you have ever spent time with someone who is a prayer warrior, you know that prayer is far from boring.

Terry is a man of faithfulness through prayer. How do I know this? Because he's my Dad. (Sorry I called you *Terry* in print, Dad!) I have seen him model a solid prayer life my whole life and inspire others to do the same. In fact, when my then-boyfriend-now-husband was asking permission to marry me years ago, my Dad told him to wait a week while he prayed about it. Dad wasn't about to give his only daughter in marriage without praying about it first! That's the kind of man he is. Dad has taught me that it is my choice to follow the Lord in prayer, and his gracious admonition in this book will encourage you to do the same.

Think of this book as more than a how-to. Think of it as an investment in the future. *I* need this message. We all do. Our prayer lives matter because the Lord will soon return and we want Him to find us about our Father's business.

"Draw near to God and He will draw near to you…" -James 4:8

-Kirsten Kline
Owner/Artistic Director of Reverence Studios

# Introduction

# Nehemiah Who?

*"The words of Nehemiah the son of Hacaliah."*
*– Nehemiah 1:1*[1]

Nehemiah is one of the great yet underrepresented figures from the Old Testament. He stands near the end of OT history, after the great stories of the Bible, including Creation, the Flood, and the Exodus. When great heroes are mentioned, the list usually places Moses and David at the top, with others such as Abraham, Elijah, and Daniel as the stars of well-known Bible stories, with Nehemiah possibly as an afterthought.

Even Nehemiah's achievements are downplayed. Moses stood down Pharaoh, David bested a giant, and Daniel survived a night in a lion's den. What did Nehemiah do? He built a wall. Oh, he also got picky about following some laws we no longer consider relevant. It is easy to overlook Nehemiah, both the man and his accomplishments.

But that would be to our detriment.

When we take the time to look more closely, we uncover in post-exilic events a giant of the faith and a tenacious prayer warrior. What praise Nehemiah receives is usually for his leadership skills, with prayer as an addendum. But the proper perspective is to reverse those factors. Nehemiah was not just a great leader who prayed; he was a devout man of prayer whom God called to lead.

An analysis of the book of Nehemiah shows that prayer permeates the book. The book begins with prayer, and it ends with prayer. Whenever Nehemiah encountered a problem, his first response was to pray, and then take the appropriate action. Prayer was his reflex reaction to any and all circumstances.

Nehemiah lived this prayer-centered life because he was a man of God. Some prayers, like the classic prayer in Nehemiah chapter one, are more formal and almost liturgical in their tone. But many of the shorter prayers are more intimate, showing a personal relationship with God. Nehemiah loved God, and it was through this love that Nehemiah sought to serve and obey God.

## How Israel Got Here

By the time of Nehemiah, Israel was quickly becoming a backwater area, a vassal nation that traded one foreign ruler for another. During Nehemiah's time, Israel was a Persian province with only a governor, not even meriting a vassal king. The fall from the lofty days of David and Solomon 500-plus years earlier was long and hard.

While idolatry had always been a problem for Israel, it had been intensified by the many foreign wives brought in by Solomon. After Solomon, when Israel split into two kingdoms, the Northern Kingdom set up altars in Dan and Bethel, which had golden calves for the people to worship. While not fully abandoning God, the Israelites adopted syncretism, the practice of blending multiple religious beliefs or appending beliefs to existing worship.[2]

> **Prayer was Nehemiah's reflex reaction to any and all circumstances.**

This practice angered God, so judgment began to fall on Israel, even as prophets were sent to warn people of the consequences of their sin. These warnings were ignored, and successive judgments became opportunities to include even more religious practices, in hopes that one of the gods might deliver them. After many years of rebellion, Israel fell. First the Northern Kingdom was conquered by Assyria and its people carried away in 722 B.C. Then the Southern Kingdom, or Judah, fell to the Babylonian Empire in successive stages of exile, finally destroying Jerusalem and the Temple in 587 B.C. The entirety of Israel had ceased to exist as an independent nation.

After a period of exile, the Israelites were permitted to return to their land and rebuild the Temple. But they were under the control of the Persian Empire and at the mercy of the people around them. Israel still suffered the after-effects of their disobedience.

Then Nehemiah entered onto the stage, about seventy-five years after the Exile. He lived in Persia, as part of the Israelite community who did not return to their homeland. He held a serving position as cupbearer to the king of Persia. While not a high-ranking or politically powerful position, it was one imbued with great trust as the man responsible for the safety of the king's food and drink. Not a king. Not a priest. Just a descendant of exiles holding a service job. This was the man that God chose for the important task of moving Israel back to their intended position.

What Nehemiah lacked in credentials or lineage was more than compensated for by his character. While we first encounter him as an adult during this moment of crisis for Israel, God had been preparing him and walking alongside him. We read of his devotion to God by how he responded to every situation that arises. We see his intimacy with God by how he talked with God in prayer. We see his zeal for God by how he responded to corruption and public sin. This kind of character strength did not appear suddenly. It was developed over years of fellowship with God.

## A Life to be Emulated

Sometimes we can observe someone and say, "I wish I had their life," or more commonly, we desire a specific trait or feature, as in, "I wish I had their _____." Nehemiah lived the kind of life that, through his prayerfulness and devotion to God, can be a positive role model for us today.

We can look at our lives and take stock of where we are. Are we happy with where we are and the direction we are traveling? Would we like to make any adjustments or attempt to move faster and progress more quickly? Or perhaps we realize we are facing the wrong direction and would like to turn around and go the other way? The Greek word translated as *repent* means *to turn* or *change direction*. Maybe we need a simple alignment, or maybe we need an entirely new course.

This book is designed to guide you toward God by rebuilding your prayer life. Perhaps you just need a little tinkering and focus, or perhaps you need an overhaul or a brand new start. Either way, the life of Nehemiah can be used as a model by which we can build and strengthen our relationship with God by growing and deepening our prayer life. Each chapter provides prayer building blocks which, if followed throughout the book, lead us toward strong fellowship with God. Just as Nehemiah rebuilt the wall by filling in the gaps and resetting the gates and doors, we can rebuild our relationship with God to be richer, deeper, and more intimate.

Nehemiah did not attain his maturity and intimacy with God quickly, developing this type of relationship takes time. We have to undo old patterns and establish new patterns. We need to resist the call of the world and embrace the call of God. We may take steps that need to be repeated and renewed in coming seasons. My prayer is that this book becomes your opportunity to launch into a vibrant and intimate relationship with God as you rebuild your prayer life and devotion to God.

# Chapter 1

# A Response to a Crisis

"Houston, we have a problem."
*— Jim Lovell*[1]

"My wife and I barely exist together. Since the loss of our child, she wants to move out to reassess our marriage, but I'm afraid that if she does, she's never coming back."

While golfing with a friend, I had ventured away from golf-centered conversation and asked how he was doing. His response obliterated my perceived reality of their lives. He added that they kept communication to a minimum because it often degenerated into conflict. He still loved his wife but did not know what to do.

Needless to say, I lost my concentration on golf that day. My already mediocre game deteriorated into pathetic flailing at the golf ball. I could not offer any profound advice or counsel to my friend, and any platitudes would have been insulting, but I encouraged him to stay together and under the same roof. I also committed with my friend to pray for him and his wife daily. We prayed at the end of the round, and I went home, reeling from what I had heard.

I had resolved to pray daily and I kept my commitment, pouring out my concern before God. Sometimes we find it difficult to discern God's will in a situation, but this was easy: God desires loving, intimate marriages centered on Him. As the months passed, I saw their relationship deteriorate further, bottom out, then begin to improve. They had renewed their life together prior to moving away. They later had another child and appeared to be in a healthy marriage.

# Crisis and Response

How do you respond to a crisis? When you encounter a desperate situation, whether involving you or someone close to you, what is your initial reaction? Do you panic? Do you rush around in an adrenaline-fueled frenzy, hoping that activity, any activity, will somehow mitigate the crisis? Do you stop to assess your situation, evaluate different courses of action, and then implement what appears to be the best alternative? Do you turn to God?

How you respond to a crisis provides insights into your priorities and heart.

You might be living your life, comfortable and with no major disruptions, confident that life is good and getting better. You might even have high hopes for the future, feeling like you can tackle any situation and overcome any problem. Then, you are hit with an unexpected punch to the gut that leaves you breathless. As you gasp to suck oxygen into your lungs, you survey the wreckage that you once considered a wonderful life.

Perhaps disaster may even strike near to you. Someone very dear is struggling and overwhelmed after being pounded by a crisis, with their future and possibly their very life in the balance. You feel prompted to intervene, but you have no idea of the right steps to take. Even if you did know the right steps, you are powerless to take any action. So you are forced to watch as someone you love is drowning in suffering.

> **How you respond to a crisis provides insights into your priorities and heart.**

Nehemiah encountered this type of problem when talking to his brother at the beginning of the book of Nehemiah. He inquired about matters in Jerusalem to see how the Jews that had returned from the Exile were doing. His brother told him that "the remnant there in the province who had survived the exile is in great trouble and shame. The wall of Jerusalem is broken down, and its gates are destroyed by fire" (Neh. 1:3).

This was the crisis that Nehemiah faced. He begins by sitting down and weeping, and then with fasting, with mourning, and with prayer. In fact, Nehemiah's standard response to any situation is with prayer. This prayer-based response, including a spontaneous prayer mid-conversation as recorded in Nehemiah 2:4, demonstrates his close relationship with God. We can learn about Nehemiah's dependency on God through his handling of the crises he encounters during the events in the book bearing his name.

## Ancient City Walls and Security

Nehemiah is overcome by the distress and danger facing his fellow Jews. He saw the city of his ancestors, the home of the Temple of his God, defenseless and vulnerable to attack. Today, we may not experience the same strong reaction as Nehemiah did to the destruction of a city's walls. In fact, we might say it was for the better, so the city could continue to expand. But to help us understand the problem this caused in ancient times, we must understand that, throughout history, the wall surrounding a city was its primary method of defense against enemies. The city wall created a place of safety and refuge for both the city inhabitants and those in nearby villages. It was difficult, if not impossible, to overtake a city using ancient weaponry. An enemy wishing to attack a walled city was forced to engage in a long and costly siege—which may or may not be successful.

The gates also allowed people and merchandise in during the day, and could then be closed and secured at night. Ancient gates were constructed with multiple rooms, or chambers, which allowed only narrow points of access to enter the city, often with a separate door to enter each chamber. Thus, it was difficult for a large force to make a rapid assault due to the narrow gate openings. This feature negated any numerical advantage held by the invading army, because the narrow space meant that just a few soldiers could enter at one time. The defenders could then repel the attack from both the front and the top of the gate.

To make assaults by enemy armies more difficult, people built most ancient cities on a large mound. They then built ramps leading to the gates along the city wall, with a sharp right turn to enter the gate. This eliminated the possibility of an army backing up and ramming the gate to force their way in. The right turn into the gate kept an enemy soldier's right hand along the wall instead of being free for combat. Also, keeping the ramp near the city wall allowed the defenders to attack the invading army while they marched up the ramp to approach the gate. An intact city wall and functioning gates were an ancient city's primary defense.[2]

But Jerusalem was vulnerable to anyone who wished to attack because the wall was broken down and the gates burned and ineffective. While the Persian Empire claimed official protection over Israel, the Persian capital was hundreds of miles away and not able to respond in a timely manner in case of attack. Just like today, plenty of people back then, such as the Samaritans and Ammonites, were ready to inflict pain and suffering on the Jews.

Of all the cities to lie exposed to attack, Jerusalem meant the most to any God-fearing Jew. The city occupied the mountain where Abraham nearly sacrificed Isaac before God provided a substitute. After David took the city from the Jebusites, he brought the Ark of the Covenant here. Jerusalem held the Temple of God, first built by Solomon to house the Ark and be God's dwelling place on earth. Jerusalem symbolized God's ongoing covenant with the people of Israel. To have the walls destroyed and the city vulnerable emphasized the broken fellowship between Israel and their God. Its wreckage was a visual reminder of a good relationship gone bad.

Nehemiah responded through a series of actions. He first reacts by sitting down. The ancient Israelites often expressed their sorrow or distress in physical actions, including sitting. To sit down demonstrated an immediate interruption of daily activities. It was a deliberate decision made to stop whatever was being done at that moment because the person was so overcome that he or she could not continue.

The dire situation also reduced Nehemiah to weeping. The word translated as *wept* means *to cry with tears*, including *wailing* and *lamenting*. The lament was a common post-exilic form of expressing distress, used in many psalms from that period. A common lament theme was "How long, O Lord?" directed at the suffering endured by the Israelites, and seeking God's mercy. Someone caught up in weeping cannot do much else, although weeping may include reaching out to God to help understand their plight.

Then, after weeping, Nehemiah mourned. Mourning is not as debilitating as weeping, but it is a long-lasting, deep pain reaching to the very heart of a person. Mourning suggests a sense of loss, of something that once was but is now gone. It is possible to still function while mourning. But rather than a quick emotional response, mourning continues for long periods of time. Nehemiah knew of the glory of Israel under kings David and Solomon, a glory that eroded and was finally obliterated under a crushing defeat by

Nebuchadnezzar and the resultant exile hundreds of miles from home in a strange land. Although the Persians allowed the Jews to return and even rebuild the Temple in Jerusalem, the prior glory had not returned. The Jews were weak and defenseless, and Nehemiah mourned this ongoing loss in addition to the current crisis.

The Israelites often connected mourning to other forms of sorrow, and Nehemiah fasted as part of his response. Fasting—the abstention from either specific or all foods for a period of time—had become part of the Jewish religious practice and even expanded in frequency during the Exile. The Israelites practiced fasting as part of worship during religious celebrations or specific times of remembrance. But fasting was also used during special times to seek God. Daniel fasted on different occasions when he wished to hear from God. Fasting symbolized the Jewish desire to deny oneself, to show submission to God's will. They desired to reconcile to God with the hope of receiving His favor.

With sitting, weeping, mourning, and fasting as preparation, Nehemiah prayed. The remainder of Nehemiah chapter one contains a summary of his prayer, which will be covered in later chapters. While the Bible mentions but does not describe the weeping, mourning, and fasting, Nehemiah's prayer is written out. The details of what Nehemiah prayed were considered important enough to record.

## Our Response and the Spectrum of Care

When we encounter a crisis, we can define our response as being somewhere along a spectrum of care. This spectrum can define how much the crisis impacts us, and therefore, the degree to which we respond. At one end, we don't care, responding "So what?" to the problem at hand. We may not use those words, but they describe the attitude of our response and lack of action. In our next level of response, we might be "interested." We may notice the crisis on an intellectual or academic level, but it has not triggered an emotional response. Because we feel no emotional response, we feel no prompting to take any action, and we do not experience any personal impact.

Moving further along the spectrum, we become "concerned." We begin to move past intellectual interest toward an emotional response to the crisis, and our concern will often motivate us to action. I learned about the plight of the children in a specific region of Africa when our church sponsored an event from World Vision. The makeshift African village constructed in our church displayed the grinding poverty and devastation from AIDS. We saw children struggling to cope with life hampered by the results of the sins of adults. Our concern grew as we experienced their plight compared to the blessings our children enjoyed growing up in America. When presented with an opportunity to help them break this destructive cycle and build a better life, our concern prompted our support. In the past, I had been interested in hearing about this ministry, but it was the increasing of our level of care from interested to concerned which moved us to action. However, this concern did not interrupt our lives, which continued as before, just that now we were supporting a child in Africa.

Further along the spectrum, we are "shaken." The crisis shakes us out of our daily routine, because its severe impact on our immediate lives demands a response. More than just being concerned, being shaken influences our response. Our level of concern compels us to become involved to help resolve the crisis. While a concerned level of care will motivate involvement, being shaken propels us to commitment, often holding us until we reach a point of resolution.

My friend's marital problems I discovered while golfing shook me. This was not a crisis about which I could shrug off caring, because it involved people close to me. Unlike overseas mission needs, I could not just write a check to meet a need and then continue my life as before. This crisis required my commitment until it was resolved. I could not start and then stop part way through. I had to stay firm until the end.

At the opposite end of the spectrum of care from "so what," we find ourselves "shaken to the core." This response to a crisis means that our lives will never be the same. We feel we must get involved and help in some fashion. We cannot stay uninvolved, but feel compelled to jump in and assist in any manner possible. In fact, our involvement rises to a commitment to not give up or rest until the crisis is past. The powerful impact of the crisis coupled with our degree of response moves us to a new place. Will this new place find us closer to or farther away from God?

The crisis at Jerusalem shook Nehemiah to the core, as displayed by his powerful response. Even while reeling in the midst of emotional distress, Nehemiah turned to God. Seeking God in prayer was Nehemiah's *first* response, not his last resort.

This pattern of first response through prayer demonstrates Nehemiah's close relationship to God. He built a foundation of intimacy with God through many years of devotion, prior to his awareness of the crisis at Jerusalem. This type of dependency on God through prayer cannot be summoned out of a prayerless life when an emergency occurs. It must be nurtured and developed through years of practiced prayerful intimacy.

---

## Seeking God in prayer was Nehemiah's first response, not his last resort.

---

The annoying thing about crises is that we know they *will* occur, but we just don't know *when*. If we could schedule all our emergencies, we could plan a careful and reasoned response, obviously saturated with prayer to help guide our steps. But the very definition of an "emergency" or "crisis" is that it hits us without any warning. The question posed to us is, what state will we find ourselves in when a crisis breaks down the door and enters our lives?

I prayed until the point of a successful resolution regarding my golfing friend, but I do not present this example as a testimony to my greatness, for even in this situation I had failures. I am a poor correspondent, and communication trailed off after we moved to separate states. I still pray for their continued marital success, but not with the consistency and fervor I felt while in the midst of the crisis. I use this example to demonstrate how our level of response will, in the long term, match our level of care. Also, our type of response will be consistent with our priorities, showing what we consider most important to us. I prayed because I felt powerless to do anything else, whereas Nehemiah prayed as his first response.

Nehemiah may have felt powerless, as well, in dealing with the problem at Jerusalem, but an examination of his life shows a prayer response even when he had other options. At times he combined prayer with other actions, but prayer was always present. Nehemiah knew that any actions he took were meaningless without first engaging his God. Nehemiah's God was not distant or on display in a building; He was present, faithful, and active, hearing Nehemiah's prayers and responding with divine wisdom and mighty power. Nehemiah had built a life of close relationship with God so that, when the crisis occurred, he was ready to respond to God first, and then allow God to determine the next steps of response.

# Prayer Building Block #1:
## Let God use your heart to drive you to your knees.

## Nehemiah could respond to God with prayer during a crisis because he already had established a pattern of response by prayer.

Nehemiah built a strong relationship with God through the years of his life, and he could turn to God in his time of distress. When under pressure, we will react within our comfort zones, rather than venturing in a new direction. Extreme stress makes it difficult to respond differently than our usual method of dealing with a crisis.

Second, how much we care about a given situation will influence how fervently we pray. We are not required to weep, but we are required to experience a deep concern that shakes us to the core. We may prefer to drift through life and not let events rattle us. On occasion our defenses are broken down and we become vulnerable to care for someone else. We invest ourselves in the outcome and desire to see God work in His mighty power. Feeling helpless and powerless to directly influence the outcome, we beseech God and plead for His intervention in this situation. Just as Jacob refused to release God until receiving His blessing, we must refuse to release God from our entreaties until the burden is lifted.

This prayer effort may continue for days, weeks, months, or even years. We cannot stop until we have seen God work. We will not always know the right answer, but we know that God needs to be present in this situation. This steadfastness, this fervency, this drive to pray until we see results, is fueled by our deep caring for the person or persons affected by the crisis at hand.

## Take a reflective look at your life and recall how you have responded to crises in the past.

- Did you pray?
- Did you panic?

- Did you weep?
- Perhaps, not knowing how to respond to the stress and pain, you numbed yourself so that your level of care lessened until you could ignore the situation.
- How much did you seek God's help in prayer rather than trying to fix the problem in your own strength?

Do not punish yourself over past failures, as we have all been AWOL from earlier battles. But with honesty and humility assess how you have dealt with past crises and confess any failure to God.

Nehemiah carried the burden of the distress of the people in Jerusalem. He felt their trouble in his heart. But he did not carry his burden alone. He took his burden to the God he already knew deeply in the form of mourning, fasting, and praying. Knowing he was powerless to fix the problem, he pleaded with God for a favorable outcome.

## Now review your present life for any crisis situations, impacting you or those close to you.

What are the greatest burdens you are currently carrying?

Even if they do not feel like catastrophic problems, begin the practice of taking everything to God in prayer, seeking to deepen your daily relationship with Him. Follow the example of Nehemiah and stop aimless worrying or fretting. Turn your concern and heartache for the situation into fervency in prayer.

Grab hold of God and do not let go.

## Chapter 2

# Snatching Defeat from the Jaws of Victory

*"My mind is set upon it [returning home] and my companions' too."*
*— Ulysses, "The Odyssey"*[1]

In the summer of 1984, Dwight Gooden faced a seemingly limitless future as the latest possessor of Major League Baseball's Golden Arm. He burst onto the scene in the early 1980s, overpowering defenseless batters with a devastating array of pitches. As strikeout totals rose to stratospheric levels, he earned one award after another. First, he won Rookie of the Year, then he earned the Cy Young Award for best pitcher. He helped propel the New York Mets to the World Series Championship in 1986. His love for the game was infectious, so that even fans of teams he defeated with ease could enjoy the artistry of his performances. A rapid start promised a legendary career with the presumed eventual enshrinement in the Hall of Fame as one of baseball's all-time greatest players.

Then an appallingly sad form of tragedy struck.

Not an arm injury, which in the past had struck down so many promising pitchers. Not a disease, sapping the energy and even life of once-strong players. Not even a mysterious loss of control, which can render the greatest pitcher completely ineffective.

No, Dwight Gooden's downfall was self-inflicted. As he reached the top of his profession, he succumbed to cocaine use. He hid his addiction briefly, but it took its toll and crippled him. In and out of drug rehab, Dwight

Gooden lost both his magic and artistry on the mound. While he eked out a career until age 35, he lost his effectiveness as a pitcher before he turned 30.

It was a shame to watch him almost willingly abandon his team and his talent to drugs and alcohol. Most fans and players would give their other arm to have half of his talent. How could he take so lightly a gift that was so unique? Watching Dwight Gooden hanging on in his later years was sad to behold, dividing emotions between watching in horror as the wreck slowly transpired and looking away to spare him the embarrassment as he thrashed around in defeat. His career had crashed, and no amount of effort could return him to his prior levels of greatness. A man blessed with rare pitching abilities threw it away because he could not conquer his addictions.

Likewise, Israel received many blessings from God. He preserved them during their years of bondage in Egypt, multiplying them from an extended family into a mighty nation. Then, in a dramatic series of miracles, He crushed Egypt for refusing to free the Israelites. This stubbornness on the part of the Egyptians culminated in a devastating loss of life to both their people and livestock.

Once Israel left Egypt, God provided safe passage through the Red Sea and cut off any opportunity of pursuit as He destroyed Pharaoh's army in the flood waters. Having secured Israel's freedom, God renewed His covenant with the descendants of Abraham, through Moses as the intermediary between the Israelites and God. Laws were given not only to define Israel's responsibilities in the covenant, but to provide the framework for building a new nation and society once Israel reached the Promised Land.

God was faithful even when Israel disobeyed. When He forced Israel to remain in the desert for 40 years because of unbelief, God continued to provide food, water, and even preserved their clothing. When Israel acted out by complaining or worshipping idols, God administered discipline but never wavered in His keeping of the covenant. God brought Israel into the Promised Land, won their battles over the current occupants, and enabled them to settle into the land He had promised them. God had set everything up for Israel, blessing them with what they needed to prosper as a nation. All they needed to do was to obey and serve God, worshipping only Him.

That must have been too much to ask of Israel in return for abundant blessings.

The book of Judges recounted a tragic cycle of Israel forsaking God, God disciplining Israel by allowing other nations to oppress them, Israel crying out in desperation, God raising up leaders to deliver Israel from her oppressors, and Israel worshipping God. Then the next generation came along, forgot what happened, forsook God and started the cycle over again. Except each time the sin became more severe, and the repentance not quite as genuine or long lasting. Instead of returning at some point to obedient worship of God, Judges chronicled a gradual decline to where the behavior of the Israelites could not be distinguished from the sinfulness of their neighboring nations.

## The Sin of Syncretism

Why was Israel unable to obey God and worship only Him, forsaking all other gods, especially the gods of the pagan peoples around them? The seed of the problem began even before Israel entered the Promised Land, as they began to intermarry with the neighboring peoples. God specifically commanded Israel to stay away from non-Israelites, not because He is racist, but to protect them from destructive pagan cultures and beliefs. Any persons coming into Israelite society from other nations, which were normally women, would bring in their own practices and religions, which would corrupt the worship of God. When unbelief prevented Israel from dislodging all the native people from the Promised Land, intermarriage continued with the local people and corruption of Israelite worship continued to fester, even as the nation grew and became a kingdom.

> God's discipline is for a season, but His mercy endures forever.

Israel never fully abandoned worship of God until near the end of the First Temple period. They practiced syncretism, the blending of multiple religious practices, rather than staking all their faith on one set of beliefs. The most common local god Israel worshipped was Baal, perceived by the Canaanites as bringing the Fall-Winter rains necessary for successful harvests in a semi-arid region.[2] They also worshipped household gods, or personal gods, those having been introduced into Israel as far back as Rachel, Jacob's wife.

I encountered a modern version of syncretism while on a business trip in India. I arrived at the office prior to the local staff my first day and perused the cubicles, looking for familiar names in an unfamiliar land. Knowing that most Indians were Hindu, I was surprised to find a plaque with the words of Joshua 24:15: "As for me and my house, we will serve the LORD." I found out that this co-worker was a practicing Hindu, yet attended a Christian worship service each week. He diligently followed what he perceived to be the beliefs of both religions, just in case one was more effective than the other. He missed the point of all religions, and especially Judeo-Christian worship, in which to be obedient is to forsake all other belief systems.

Yet Israel persisted in this same syncretic belief pattern, even after repeated rebuke and discipline from God. Jeroboam, the first ruler of the Northern Kingdom, set up golden calves in Dan and Bethel so that the newly independent tribes of Israel would not worship in Jerusalem. Ahab's wife Jezebel attempted to eradicate worship of God within Israel by expanding Baal worship. God used the prophet Hosea as an object lesson to warn Israel about impending judgment due to unfaithfulness, but the warnings went unheeded, and Israel subsequently was conquered.[3] Even after God exiled the Northern Kingdom due to disobedience, the remaining tribes continually rejected God in favor of idol worship. There were periods of revival, highlighted by the reforms of kings Hezekiah and Josiah, but Israel persisted in forsaking God.

After repeated prophecies and warnings, God finally could not withhold judgment any longer, and He allowed the remaining tribes to be conquered and Jerusalem and the Temple to be destroyed by the Babylonians. The leaders of Israelite society were taken into captivity and the land left barren. Even at this stage, God promised a time of future restoration through Jeremiah and others. God's discipline is for a season, but His mercy endures forever.

## A Return without Full Restoration

During the Exile, Israel finally did away with idol worship and outward syncretism. A strong commitment to the Law was reestablished, including additional regulations which placed "a law around the Law" to keep the nation from sinning through disobedience to the Law. Spiritual disciplines, including keeping the Sabbath and an increased emphasis on

Snatching Defeat from the Jaws of Victory

prayer, emerged and became more prominent during this time.[4] But the new practices were not the same as heartfelt, surrendered obedience to God.

After the Exile, Israel was granted the right to return to their homeland by the Persian emperor Cyrus. He even permitted them the freedom to rebuild their ruined Temple, and Israel resumed their sacrificial system. Yet the religious practice seemed hollow and forced, going through the motions and maintaining the façade of worship without the complete surrender God desired from His people.

The shattered potential and unrealized glory Dwight Gooden experienced on a personal basis was being lived out at a national level by Israel, but with their efforts at restoration falling short. Each new effort to do the right thing to please God was another reminder that they were in fact *not* pleasing God. Each new step to reestablish worship patterns betrayed the truth that they favored form over substance. Each new round of sacrificial offerings demonstrated that they withheld from God what He desired most, their hearts. In all their religious activity, they never took the very action God wanted: surrender.

## A Shadow of Its Former Self

Israel had been allowed by Cyrus to return to its home and rebuild the Temple. They resumed worship in Jerusalem, and yet what was experienced could not be construed in any way as a full restoration to its former glory. Israel still lived under the thumb of a foreign ruler, forced to pay tribute and give allegiance to an outside kingdom. Local peoples harassed the Jews and were ready to attack should Israel show any signs of casting off her bonds. Jerusalem lay defenseless, the walls broken and the gates burned.

Israel had squandered the blessings generously given by God, and now the people lived in servitude. There may have been people like Nehemiah, who were individually successful and secure, but any security was dependent on the wishes of their Persian masters. The Jews

> Before Israel could move towards God, they had to first understand how far away from God they were in their current situation.

remaining in exile existed as second-class citizens, far from their homeland, and those who returned to Israel lived in poverty and fear.

This is the world in which Nehemiah found himself when presented by the crisis of Jerusalem lacking a defensible wall. Israel was controlled by foreign nations and unable to determine her own destiny. They resumed temple worship, and many people had ceased directly worshipping other gods. But many Jews had also become comfortable in their lives in exile, and seemed willing to "settle" for a safe and decent life over the unknown of following God. Not having personally experienced God's blessings, they were content to improvise the best they could outside of God's Promised Land.

Although Nehemiah was also living the life of an exile, and had carved out a somewhat secure life as cupbearer to the Persian king, he knew God wanted more for His chosen people than a life of superficial worship and bondage. God wanted devoted followers on which He could bestow bountiful blessings. But before Israel could move towards God, they had to first understand how far away from God they were in their current situation. What choices had Israel made which brought them to their current situation? They needed to realize how far they had strayed from God's original plan for their nation *before* they could begin the journey back to where God intended them to be all along.

## Where Are We?

It is easy to look back from our perspective in history and condemn Israel, criticizing their lack of faith and willful worship of other gods. Yet do we not ourselves take matters into our own hands rather than waiting on God's deliverance and plan to come into fruition? We decide to play it safe and set up a backup plan in case God does not come through, which we quickly put into action since we cannot wait on God. Once our plan produces poor results, we keep trying to dig ourselves out of our problems rather than repenting and turning back to God. Our continued failure makes us double down on our efforts, producing a downward spiral into sin and defeat. We suddenly awaken one day to realize that we are a long way from where God intended us to be. Without erecting a single statue, we have practiced modern-day syncretism by combining worship of God with other things, including our own efforts independent of God.

God desires to bring victory into our lives, but we block His efforts with our own unbelief and unfaithfulness. We make brief efforts to follow God but give up before any lasting progress is made, discouraged by a lack of immediate reward. We don't realize it is often our own lack of faith that hampers God from working in our lives, so we misinterpret the silence or distance as God not being responsive to our needs. We then look to our own methods to conquer the problems in our life, continually digging ourselves into a deeper hole while tearing down the walls God uses to protect us from outside attacks.

We continue this self-focused downward pattern until we either hit a crisis or reach the end of our own efforts with no relief in sight. Like the ancient Israelites, we need to understand just how far we have moved from God's plan. What specific actions did we take, what specific decisions did we make, that brought us to the place we are today?

> Like the ancient Israelites, we need to understand just how far we have moved from God's plan.

Twelve-step programs generally make self-recognition as step one. Before anyone can begin a path towards healing, they must first admit they are powerless over whatever self-destructive behavior or addiction is controlling them. Until people realize that they cannot fix themselves, they will not turn to anyone else for help. We prefer to be self-reliant, even in our failure. But until addicts admit they are powerless to conquer their addictions, they are unable to progress in any recovery program.

Israel needed to come to the same conclusion: they could not achieve God's will and plan for their nation in their own strength. They would not be ready to surrender to God for help until they knew just how far they had forsaken their covenant with Him.

Likewise, we must recognize our current position with God. Just how close are we to God? How much effort do we put into our relationship with Him? Have we made any specific decisions that drove a wedge between us and our Heavenly Father?

# Prayer Building Block #2:
## Understand how you arrived at your current state.

**Israel turned from God and entered into syncretism and sin because they stopped depending on Him.**

Subsequent generations had not personally experienced His deliverance and grew distant from their Provider. That distance became unbelief, which manifested into God not working in their lives because they refused to look for Him to work in their lives, or they refused to accept God's plan over their own agenda.

By the time of Nehemiah, Israel existed as a second-class, defeated people, under control of others and unable to defend herself from enemy attack. Part of Nehemiah's weeping over the fate of Jerusalem was knowing that the problem was self-inflicted due to sin. Israel had chosen a path which led to defeat and exile. Israel had brought herself to her current lowly state.

## Take stock of your current relationship with God.

- Is God close to or distant from you?
- Do you depend on God, living a life of daily surrender?

Or

- Do you attempt to make your life work without reliance on God?

The most important thing you can do at this stage is to clearly understand the nature of your relationship with God. Some of you will feel comfortable in your relationship with God, but recognize that you desire to continually draw closer to Him and are ready to take the next steps. Some will recognize that, while you were once close to God, you have drifted away and are in need of turning back. Some may realize that, while admiring or even loving God, you have never taken the step of seeking salvation in Christ to reconcile and surrender yourself to Him. If this is you, please take the time right now by following these steps:

- Recognize that you have sinned and fallen short of God's will and plan for your life.

- Pray the following prayer (either word-for-word, or the ideas): "Lord, I know that I have sinned. I do not deserve Your love, but I seek Your grace. I believe that Jesus Christ died on the cross to pay the penalty for my sins, and I put my full trust in Him. I want Jesus to be Lord of my life, to follow Him from this day forward, obeying You every day."

- Begin telling others of your decision, seeking guidance, support, and fellowship with other Christians.

Nehemiah knew Israel's history and reason for being in exile. He knew that decisions made by former leaders pulled the nation from God and drove them into punishment and exile. He fully understood what had been done in the past to bring Israel to its present position.

# Now, review your life for any decisions you have made (or not made) in the past that have either brought you closer to God or pushed God further out of your life.

Recognize fully and honestly your current state regarding your relationship with God. Closely examine your life and determine how well your present situation aligns to God's plan for your life.

Know where you are in relationship to God.

# Rebuilding

# Chapter 3

# God is God and We are Not

*"Gentlemen, this is a football."*
*— Vince Lombardi, NFL Football Coach*[1]

It seemed ludicrous, almost insulting, to feel the need to point out the obvious, especially to men who had dedicated their lives to achieving excellence in the sport of American football. Yet Vince Lombardi began training camp every year with this speech. According to Jerry Kramer's book *Instant Replay*, he also used it on at least one occasion midseason when he felt the team needed to refocus. Not much of a speech as far as length goes. Not even a long sentence. Just five words. But it told them everything they needed to know.

The key to the success of Vince Lombardi's teams—and they were successful, easily winning the first two Super Bowls—was their emphasis on fundamentals. They did not try to outwit the other team, or baffle them with trick plays. They learned their jobs very well and challenged the other team to do better. They knew who they were and what they needed to accomplish. They also knew who they were not.

Beginning the season with a simple declaration of the central piece of the game reminded the team to begin with the basics. Despite all the complexities of sophisticated schemes and instant recognition of subtle pattern changes that signify a different play, football comes down to a simple premise. Your team must move the football across the other team's goal line while preventing the other team from moving the ball across *your* goal line.

# Who Are We?

With that short speech, Vince Lombardi accomplished what was needed. He began by treating them with respect, addressing them as "gentlemen." He did not belittle them or tear them down. They had intrinsic value by means of their existence.

He quickly changed gears to the point of his lesson. It may seem like stating the obvious, but there is much beneath the surface. This statement reinforced the lesson that they would never reach a place where they knew everything, where they could forget the lessons learned while developing their skills. Just as skilled musicians spent time practicing their scales, these football players needed to continually apply themselves to mastering their fundamental skills.

The most important lesson was a declaration of being: they were not the football. While this may seem like stating the obvious, this statement also declared that they were not the central point of the game. They might possess the football, or protect the person with the football, but they could never be the football. Despite all their ability and dedication, the game was not about them. It was about the football. The result was respect and humility rolled into one short declaration.

> We must grasp who God is, because our opinion of God will influence our prayers.

As we begin our prayer as part of our drawing back to God, we must also combine respect and humility as we encounter God. We must recognize who we are, which includes an understanding of who we are not. But foremost, we must grasp who *God* is, because our opinion of God will influence our prayers. After all, is this God worthy to hear our prayers? How do we address a Being that we do not fully understand?

# God of Heaven

Nehemiah began his prayer in Nehemiah 1:5 with a simple declaration: "O LORD God of heaven." This declaration meant everything in acknowledging fundamental truths about the nature of God and man.

First, Nehemiah declared that God is *LORD*. The original Hebrew was rendered *Yahweh*, or *YHWH*, and was considered to be the name of God. It makes sense to address someone by his or her name, but many Jews believe God's very name to be sacred, so they instead will use the term *hashem*, which means *the name*.

But the translation into the English *LORD* also carries meaning, as it denotes a relative position. A lord was master of a region, which gave both privilege and responsibility. The lord controlled the people and resources of the area, yet he was also in charge of their safety and well-being. There was a master-servant relationship between the lord and his people. So, the very name of God denotes a higher position and places us in a lower relative position.

Next, Nehemiah used the generic term *God*, or *Elohim*. It is capitalized to show that it is meant for YHWH and not any other god, but the character qualities of a god are understood to be possessed by YHWH as well. A *god* is a being considered to be so much more eternal, powerful, and wise than mortal humans that an attempt at comparison is impossible. Gods are on such a higher level of being that we cannot even fully comprehend them. By connecting *Elohim* to YHWH, Nehemiah asserted that YHWH possessed the attributes of a god and was in fact a god.

Further, Nehemiah included the point of reference "of heaven." This distinguished Yahweh from other gods on two levels. Most gods were tied to a given locality. They might be the god of the Amorites, or the god of the Philistines, but they were connected to a people or region. Declaring Yahweh as the God of Heaven placed Him on an entirely different plane, transcendent above people and geography. This descriptor also placed Yahweh above any other gods. Most pantheons held a hierarchy of deities, with the highest-ranking member residing in heaven. Nehemiah does not necessarily believe in a multitude of gods, but by this declaration asserts that Yahweh is above any other god that may exist.

The point of this detail is that gods were still tied to people and places during Nehemiah's time, and the relative strength of a god would be correlated to the prosperity of his people in comparison to other people. If Yahweh was connected to the people and land of Israel, it could be said that He was either impotent or indifferent. Either the Israelite attempts to worship and appease Yahweh had failed and their outcome was of no concern, or Yahweh was too weak to compete against the other gods in protecting and providing for the people of Israel.

Finally, in his prayer Nehemiah recognized that he was God's servant. There was no attempt to approach God as an equal. Nehemiah fully understood his relationship with God and the relative positions of power and authority. This lord-servant relationship also included the people of Israel, with Nehemiah as their representative.

But Nehemiah took a different approach. He acknowledged Israel's sin as the factor behind Yahweh's lack of help, which was common for the time and will be covered more in chapter five of this book. Then Nehemiah defined and declared his God to be above any other god that may exist, which was also common in that day as people would boast of the prowess of their gods. But then he took a radical departure from the theology of the day. Nehemiah declared that the evidence of Yahweh's power was not based on the prosperity of His chosen people. Yahweh's supremacy was self-evident, a facet of His very Being. Nehemiah did not need to make the case for Yahweh being Lord God of heaven. Yahweh simply *is*.

This assertion of character qualities or traits unconnected to any specific action is profoundly different from other religious practices. It is what we call praise, and centered on God's personhood and not what He has done. It was radical back then, and in our results-oriented culture, it is radical today.

# The Names of God

"LORD God of Heaven" is just one of many ways to refer to God. There are many names by which God is called in the Bible. Comforter, Almighty God, God of Jacob, Redeemer, Wonderful Counselor, Heavenly Father, and Provider are just a small sample. Each one declares or describes one attribute of God's person or character. No one descriptor can capture all of God, and even all of the names combined cannot encompass all of God. He is beyond our comprehension.

But these different names help us to get a grip on who God is, to have within our limited frame of reference a beginning understanding of the nature of God. As we contemplate these attributes, we begin to grasp the goodness and greatness of God. We recognize that God is far greater and better than we can ever dream to be. We reach the conclusion that God is on such a higher plane that it is only by His revelation of Himself that we can even have a glimpse of His being. A rational sentient being cannot help but be compelled to praise such a superior Being.

When we refer to God in different ways, it is not a confusion of identity. In fact, variety is good, because it helps us remember the many attributes of God, rather than focusing on just a few. Our love and understanding of God will grow as we deepen our awareness of the many facets of His goodness and greatness. The names of God provide handholds through which we can grasp a piece of God's character in a degree that does not overwhelm us, so that we might return our comprehension of His Person in the form of praise.

## A Great and Awesome God

We can diminish words through overuse. A word that once conveyed a powerful sentiment can be cheapened by being thrown around like confetti at a parade. Such is the plight of *awesome.*

The word once meant that which struck awe into those experiencing the presence of those it touched, a deep and reverential fear, the profound knowledge that the one feeling the awe was in the presence of something or someone who was far greater. Now the word connotes a pleasurable feeling, as in, "that ice cream was awesome." Through using it to describe any and every positive event in our lives, we have robbed it of its power to convey its original intent, the sense of fearful respect.

So, when in Nehemiah 1:5 Yahweh is referred to as "the great and awesome God," the phrase does not pack the wallop to today's reader it was intended to deliver.

Have you ever had an experience that was so overwhelming you could not continue, you had to simply stop and try to absorb what you were seeing? Years ago, my family visited Yosemite National Park for the first time. After leaving the agricultural valley, we spent miles climbing the foothills. The foothills grew into mountains, and the ravines grew larger and steeper. The higher we climbed, the higher the mountains rose up around us. Finally, we rounded a curve that placed Yosemite Valley on display. The stark granite peaks of El Capitan on the left and the Three Sisters on the right rose above the gently rounded base lushly carpeted with evergreen trees. Spectacular waterfalls cascaded off the mountain cliffs on each side and, in the back of the valley, Half Dome stood guard. Rock, water, and tree all blended to form a magnificent wilderness panorama. Wonder impressed us into silence.

Visiting the National Mall in Washington, D.C., for the first time can create a similar experience. The best effect is provided by standing near the Washington Monument. Facing the White House, the Mall stretches to the right, past the massive Smithsonian Institution buildings, dwarfing the dinosaurs displayed by the Natural History museum. At the right end, the Capitol with its magnificent dome rises up. To the left, the ground slopes down to the World War II Memorial and then the Reflecting Pool. At the left end, an incredibly broad set of steps leads up to the Lincoln Memorial, where an oversized statue of Lincoln watches over the daily proceedings. The magnitude of history combined with the people and events commemorated in one area can be heart-stopping.

> The most awe-producing effect we can experience on earth is only a hint of the awesomeness of God.

These are examples of modern-day experiences that can produce true awe, in which we are compelled to stop and reflect upon what we are seeing and experiencing. When Nehemiah refers to God as "great and awesome," he is stating that contemplating the very person and character of God produces this same response. Except that, because God is so much greater than anything in His creation, the awe effect will be so much greater. The most awe-producing effect we can experience on earth is only a hint of the awesomeness of God.

## A God of Justice and Integrity

It used to be that a man's word was good and reliable. Written contracts were primarily insurance against unknown or unscrupulous people seeking to swindle others. But these days, it seems that even contracts do not prevent people from keeping their promises, with great efforts being made to weasel out of commitments. Integrity has become so outdated that it is a refreshing throwback to encounter someone who simply keeps their word without fuss or excuse.

That is the nature of the God whom Nehemiah served, and he declared so in his prayer. A covenant in the Old Testament was a contract between God and His chosen people Israel. The entire book of Deuteronomy describes details of the original covenant established at Mount Sinai, but can be summed up in this: God would watch over, protect, and prosper the nation of Israel, and the people would remain true to God, worshipping only Him and obeying His commandments. It also included the blessings the people would experience from keeping the covenant—and the penalties incurred from breaking the covenant.

At no point does the contract stipulate penalties God would experience from breaking His side of the covenant, nor was it necessary. God embodied integrity as one of His attributes. Nehemiah referred to God as the One "who keeps covenant and steadfast love with those who love him and keep his commandments" (Neh. 1:5). This was a simple declaration of God's character, not a hopeful wish.

**Nehemiah did not need to make the case for Yahweh being Lord God of heaven. Yahweh simply is.**

The bulk of the Old Testament recounts Israel breaking their side of the covenant through worshipping other gods, flagrantly violating God's commands, or both. God patiently tried to bring Israel back before having to enact judgment upon them. But, even in judgment, God displays integrity because He is simply carrying out the conditions of the contract as a means to prod Israel into fulfilling their side of the agreement.

By the time of Nehemiah, God's justice, integrity, and love were clearly known. While God had judged the people by sending them into exile, He had never abandoned them. God had remained true to all His promises to that point, even His promise of punishing sin and rebellion. Because God had remained true and steadfast to this point in history, Nehemiah and others had every reason to trust that God would continue to keep His promises going forward.

# Prayer Building Block #3:
## Praise is our natural response to the Person of God.

## How well do you know God?

- Have you heard about Him, and possibly read about Him?
- Are you in a relationship with Him and beginning to get to know Him?
- As you seek to know God, are you realizing that God is greater than we can possibly comprehend?

It is impossible to fully grasp all that God is. However, learning about God's character attributes can help us understand His person. Because we have already experienced similar (if inferior) versions of these character qualities and attributes, we can start to piece together the person of God as revealed to us.

Nehemiah knew God and declared knowledge of God. In a few brief words, Nehemiah was able to state the essence of God as it related to himself. But this praise was not intended to massage God's ego or manipulate God into doing what Nehemiah wanted. He praised God because praise was the natural response to understanding the person of God in relation to himself.

## How do you address God today?

What do you acknowledge about God's person and character? The degree to which you truly know God will affect how you address God, as either a comparative stranger or as someone close enough to God to grasp His true nature.

Our willful, prideful selves do not easily admit to anyone greater than us, whether it be a higher level of skill in a specific area or an entirely higher level of Being. Yet we cannot honestly view the universe without coming to the realization that, by a long shot, we are not the highest form of consciousness in existence. We need to declare God's greatness in the form of praise, not because God needs to hear it, but because we need the constant reminder.

Yet as we follow this understanding and come to know this Being, we learn that His awesomeness and greatness is not to be feared and avoided, but embraced. His consistency and integrity mean He will be reliable and faithful. His justice and mercy mean that the assessment of our lives will be fair yet flavored with the intent of bringing us into a relationship that we do not deserve.

Praise God for Who He is. It is a constant reminder to you of His Person.

Rebuilding

# Chapter 4

# We are Not Alone

"Our nada who art in nada, nada be thy name
thy kingdom nada thy will be nada
in nada as it is in nada.
Give us this nada our daily nada
and nada us our nada
as we nada our nadas
and nada us not into nada
but deliver us from nada;
pues nada."
— *Ernest Hemingway*[1]

Ernest Hemingway lived the macho life about which other men could only dream: renowned writer, hunter, and all-around adventurer. He traveled the globe and wrote of his escapades in an age when most people journeyed no farther than one hundred miles from the place of their birth. He sailed ships, volunteered for wars, bagged big game, and loved women at a frenetic pace. His life as portrayed was the envy of most observers. But apparently not in his own estimation.

Ernest Hemingway ended his own life in 1961.

While all suicides are tragic, we naturally wonder at how someone who spent a lifetime living life so exuberantly could decide that their life was not worth continuing. What was the inner turmoil wreaking havoc on a life that gave every outward impression of incredible success?

Hemingway's own writing may provide some insight. The above quote, from one of his short stories, takes The Lord's Prayer and substitutes the key words with *nada*, Spanish for *nothing*. Did Hemingway reach into a spiritual darkness and, instead of finding a connection, experience a void? Did he come to believe the prayer of nothingness written in his story?

## Is Anybody Out There?

Do we believe we are alone, that we are praying to *nada*? One of the worst feelings we can experience is the sense of aloneness, the feeling that no one has our back. In the movie *Signs*, Mel Gibson plays a pastor (Graham Hess) suffering from a crisis of faith following the tragic death of his wife. When they are trapped in their house and the situation is bleak, his brother-in-law asks if they are alone or if there is a Someone looking out for them in their troubles. Hess' response? "There is no one looking out for us. We are all alone."[2] What a bleak and desperately lonely outlook on life!

Everyone faces troubles and trials during life, some more severe than others. During those times, do we feel alone, or do we feel Someone is watching over us? Do we feel that we have to face life's struggles in our own strength?

Perhaps the only experience more lonely than feeling that no one is there is believing that Someone is there, but He does not care. He may have the means to look out for us, but have no interest in doing so. Hemingway often expressed that viewpoint in his writing, showing nature as a cruel antagonist which if it was a personal being, delighting in tormenting mortal men. This fear of loneliness and abandonment can be summarized in two questions: Is God there, and does He care?

## Please Hear Me

Nehemiah fully believed in God, or why else did he pray and fast? But the ancient non-Israelite cultures did not believe in a loving God. Their gods were capricious beings who needed to be bribed and cajoled into responding positively to human requests. Systems of sacrifice and debasement were used to manipulate their gods into the desired actions. These methods of appeasement too easily bled into Israelite religious practice.

Yahweh did not need this type of manipulation, and Nehemiah did not stoop to this pagan practice. But he also knew that God had punished His people for disobedience, and would not hear the cries of a sinful, unrepentant people. Was God ready to listen after years of repentance and attempts to reform worship? Nehemiah sought God's attention before continuing into the needs behind the reason for prayer.

First, Nehemiah asked that God's "ear be attentive" (Neh. 1:6). It does not matter if someone is speaking if the other person is not listening. In our current world, constant background noise can block what we are saying so that no one can hear us. Or, if someone is not paying attention to us, our words blend in with the other background noise and are lost. To have someone's attentive ear means that they are pushing through any competing noises to hear what we have to say. That was what Nehemiah sought from God.

> To have someone's attentive ear means that they are pushing through any competing noises to hear what we have to say.

Second, Nehemiah asked that God's "eyes be open to hear the prayer" (Neh. 1:6). How do *eyes* hear a prayer when that would normally be the job of the *ears*? In the movie *Beyond the Sea*, Bobby Darin is portrayed later in his career being ignored and almost booed from the stage, even when performing songs that had been big hits. When he sought advice, he was told that *people hear what they see.* Darin had changed his appearance from the tuxedo-clad crooner of the late 1950s to resemble the long-haired counter-culture music scene of the 1960s. Although the voice was the same, the audience did not connect his voice with his new appearance. Once he returned to his prior look, the audiences again received him warmly. Rick Nelson expressed a similar experience with his new appearance drowning out familiar words for an unreceptive audience in his song "Garden Party."

The point of these examples is that what we see will often influence what we hear. God already knows our hearts and can look past our appearances. But our efforts will often show in ourselves the changes He already knows. Nehemiah wanted God to see what was being done in conjunction with prayer to ensure God's positive attention. Nehemiah had already been fasting, mourning, and praying before beginning his prayer. He then continued with what he wanted God to presently see as worthy of His attention. This does not mean Nehemiah was bribing or appeasing God, but that Nehemiah, as a changed person, was indicative of a changed people who were ready to return to fellowship with God.

Third, Nehemiah recognized that he was God's servant. There was no attempt to approach God as an equal. Nehemiah fully understood his relationship with God and the relative positions of power and authority. This lord-servant relationship also included the people of Israel, with Nehemiah as their representative.

Fourth, Nehemiah pointed out that he had been praying "before [God] day and night" (Neh. 1:6). In chapter one, the urgency of Nehemiah's response is described. That urgency had not faded, with Nehemiah defining himself as praying continually. This is not a casual interest or prayer of convenience. He showed his commitment and seriousness through his steadfast prayer.

Finally, Nehemiah announced the beneficiaries of his prayer, "the people of Israel your servants" (Neh. 1:6). He did not want God to think this effort was self-serving. While Nehemiah was himself an Israelite, he focused on his entire nation. He sought to have the whole *nation* blessed by God. But he first took these steps to make sure that God was listening to his plea. He hoped that God would see devotion and obedience, and therefore hear the subsequent prayer.

When my children were younger, they knew they needed to get my full attention to ensure I was listening. They quickly learned that, if I was distracted but heard them, I could easily mutter a response without really hearing them and engaging with them. So, if I was watching television, they would stand between me and the TV before they began speaking. If I was reading, they would gently lower the book or magazine with their hand before they engaged me. They wanted both my eyes and my ears. They knew if they had my eyes they would also have my ears. They knew I would be attentive if distractions were removed.

# In Pursuit of God

We must never forget that God strongly desires relationship. Some theologians state that a benefit of the Trinity is that God can be in relationship with Himself, consisting of three Persons. But the requirement for any relationship is that the desire for relationship must be reciprocal. One-sided relationships do not last. Unbalanced relationships where one party is too eager to engage with even minimal effort from the other party will not be healthy and not likely last. So how does a God who loves us beyond our comprehension and strongly desires to be in a relationship with us help build a healthy relationship with us?

The parable of the Prodigal Son is often taught to show us God's overwhelming love and forgiveness. The song "When God Ran" by Benny Hester describes the great immovable God running to one of His children. But both the parable and the song highlight the condition of God's running: the *repentance* of the prodigal. The father stayed where he was and waited for the lost child to return. Once the child made the effort to return, the father joyously ran to restore and rebuild the relationship.

Does God *need* us? No, He is complete within Himself. We need to know that we must also pursue God even as He pursues us. We must demonstrate, perhaps more to ourselves since God already knows our hearts, that we *want* and *need* to be in relationship with God. We must take the necessary steps from our side of the relationship to seek and find God.

# Knowing God

Nehemiah understood the importance of knowing God, not just manipulating Him to perform as desired. The history of Israelite religious practice shows a shift from ceremonial and outward worship to more personal and inward religious experience. While some, like David, were earlier outliers who knew the heart of God, the practice of inward worship grew during the later prophets such as Jeremiah. After the destruction of the Temple, there could be no outward sacrifice and national worship, so the emphasis of personal relationship with God accelerated during the Exile. By Nehemiah's time, Temple worship had been restored, but the practice of personal relationship to God over and above corporate worship remained.

Nehemiah may have used formal words, but he expressed a personal relationship with God. Defining himself as God's servant positioned Nehemiah in a subservient relationship with God. Describing God—who is Spirit and could not be cast in any physical image—as having eyes and ears made Him personal rather than an indistinct force. As will be seen in later chapters, Nehemiah speaks to God in a personal manner. The tone is not ceremonial so much as it is relational.

Then, Nehemiah finished his prayer with another plea for God to hear him: "O Lord, let your ear be attentive to the prayer of your servant, and to the prayer of your servants who delight to fear your name" (Neh. 1:11). But while he again seeks God's ear, different aspects are emphasized.

First, Nehemiah asked that God's "ear be attentive" (Neh. 1:11). Classes are often given on the distinction between passive listening and active listening. While passive listening involves no effort, active listening requires full engagement of the hearer. There may be comments or clarifying questions, but the hearer will be fully attuned to the speaker. Nehemiah sought God's full attention and hopeful action from the prayer, not just acknowledgement that the words were received.

> We must demonstrate that we want and need to be in relationship with God.

Second, Nehemiah restated his relationship to God. He and the people of Israel were servants of the Lord. This was a reminder to God that they understood their position in the relationship.

Finally, Nehemiah emphasized to God that he and his people "delight to fear your name" (Neh. 1:11). This relationship was not just for convenience or favors; they wanted the relationship with God. While Nehemiah naturally hoped for a benefit from his relationship with God, the prayer stressed the knowledge and importance of the relationship itself while acknowledging that God was superior to them. They had purposely changed their behavior in pursuit of the relationship with God. Nehemiah had dedicated himself to fasting and prayer day and night in demonstration of his desire to know God. He knew God existed and was present in the lives of the Israelites. Nehemiah wanted his relationship with God to succeed.

# To Whom are we Praying?

Do we live our lives as if God exists and is active, or are we practical atheists? It is easy to verbally assert allegiance to God, but in a crisis, to whom or what do we turn? Have we moved so far away from God that when we reach out in desperation we touch nada? Or perhaps we are defeated before we even start, refusing to even seek God out of fear that He might reject us?

It seems Ernest Hemingway apparently found nothing, as he reached a point where he found his life not worth living. We know from historical accounts that Hemingway's health was plagued with problems that were not entirely of his own making, and these may have contributed to his death. But what else may have lingered in his mind? Nehemiah, however, sought God with all his heart, desiring for the Lord to hear him and be attentive to his requests. Which example points to a better, more hopeful life? Which model has our lives more closely resembled to this point?

The prodigal son rejected his father, only to realize the folly of his ways and turn back to renew relationship with his father, even in the position of a servant. The son's desire to restore the relationship superseded any demand he might claim to a title or position. He was ready to lower himself to the level of a servant to renew his relationship with his father.

Nehemiah knew he and the Israelites were servants and not equals, and that due to sin even their position as servants was due to the grace of God. But he also knew that God was ready to hear, ready to be attentive, ready to bless. Israel had to demonstrate that they were ready to fully engage in the relationship. They would not be seeking God just for favors. They would be seeking fellowship with God.

We can follow the example of Ernest Hemingway, whose writings do not imply that he sought God, and he eventually blinked in the face of seeming nothingness, snuffing out his own life. Or we can follow the example of Nehemiah, wholeheartedly pursuing God with all that we have to offer. Which example is less likely to generate feelings of abandonment and loneliness? Which example is more likely to experience God and be known by God? Who is more likely to be heard by God and blessed by God?

# Prayer Building Block #4:
## God is there to hear us, but we must seek Him.

## How vigorously are you pursuing your relationship with God?

Is it one-sided, where God works hard to get your attention, yet you don't really care? Is it lopsided, where you might give God a little attention if He blesses you sufficiently? Are you seeking God but frustrated by the difficulty of maintaining a relationship with a Being who is only Spirit and cannot be seen or touched? Or are you enjoying a healthy and reciprocal relationship with God in Jesus Christ?

Nehemiah understood the relationship between himself and God. He knew his position as servant, and his still-formal language reflected the distinct flavor of a relationship between a physical being and a spiritual Being. Yet the differences increased rather than dampened his fervor in pursuing God.

## What are you doing in your life today to pursue your relationship with God?

What are you doing to get God's attention, to make His ears attentive and His eyes open to hear you? Just as the degree of a crisis will determine the urgency of our response, the degree of our desire to know God will determine the urgency with which we pursue God.

Take stock of your life, and the priority to which you give your relationship with God. Are you taking time to be with God? Does He ever get your undivided attention, or do daily distractions intrude on any scraps of time tossed in His direction?

## Are you even looking for God in the right place?

Sometimes we get discouraged and feel God is not listening, when what is happening is that we seek God in the wrong place or in the wrong way. The prodigal son could not find his father in just any place; he had to return to the father's home. If we have built a false construct of God, we could be needlessly expending our energy seeking God where He never was meant to be found. If we have left God, we must return to where we departed and not go somewhere else.

But do not ever doubt God's desire to be in relationship with you, or desire to hear you or be attentive to you. Just as with the prodigal son, God is ready to run to you once you turn your heart toward Him. He is ready to embrace you, to make you His child, and to hear your needs and cries. God's love for you drives His desire to know you and be known by you.

But you must also want to know God and be known by God.

# Rebuilding

# Chapter 5

# Seeking Forgiveness

"We have met the enemy and he is us."
– Pogo[1]

How do you help someone who is caught in a cycle of failure, yet unaware that they are causing their own continuing demise? In his book, *Good to Great*, Jim Collins describes what he calls the Doom Loop, which consists of four steps: 1) disappointing results, 2) reaction without understanding, 3) new direction, program, leader, fad, or acquisition, and 4) no buildup and no accumulated momentum. While this analysis was done on businesses, it can also apply to other organizations and individual people. Note step three. It was not that nothing was done in the midst of failure. In fact, a flurry of activity can mask a sinking ship or failing situation.[2]

The ancient Israelites were very busy religiously, even as they were experiencing God's judgment. As each step of judgment came to pass, they worked even harder and offered more sacrifices to God. They even offered sacrifices to *other* gods, in case one of *them* was the offended deity. As each round of punishment intensified, they added more laws to the existing laws, and in some cases, sacrificed their own children to show their zeal in appeasing whoever was responsible for their downward spiral. But their efforts were all futile because they suffered the symptom mentioned in step two of the Doom Loop: they had no understanding of the reason behind their suffering.

In other words, they were clueless.

# Recognition is the First Step

The Israelites took the wrong steps because they had diagnosed the wrong problem. They thought they were being punished for a lack of zeal in worship, or an insufficient amount of sacrifices made. It was only after being exiled that understanding came, and even then they had only partial understanding.

They knew they had broken the Law introduced as part of the Covenant with Moses on Mt. Sinai. So the exilic leadership built a "law around the Law," a set of injunctions that either were stricter than the laws God had given them, or described in meticulous detail how to keep the law. Their reasoning was that these additional regulations would provide a sufficient buffer so that people would not break the law. But because their zeal to obey God was misguided, their effort to please God was misplaced.

God never intended to keep score on a massive spreadsheet of laws and regulations. Once Israel fixated on the law, they lost track of what God wanted from the beginning. For although the Covenant was written in a format similar to the political contracts of the day, God never planned to interact with Israel in a businesslike manner. He desired a *relationship* with His people.

> The Israelites were taking the wrong steps because they had diagnosed the wrong problem.

This does not mean that the Law was unimportant or did not need to be followed. It means that Israel got their priorities backwards in dealing with God. They focused on the Law and feared God's wrath if they broke the law. Yet God wanted a relationship built on love and dedication, with obedience to the Law as a demonstration of that love.

Even today, some Christians can focus on following a set of rules rather than focusing on intimacy with God. How could it be said that Jesus came to both fulfill and abolish the Law? Because God's plan was never to have just a legal relationship with His people, but to have a personal relationship expressed with legal parameters. So when we break our side of the agreement, it is not just a legal matter, it is a personal affront to God.

# All Sin is Against God

When we want to get someone's attention, we will lead with what we consider to be most important for them to hear once we have their attention. When he was seeking God's ear, Nehemiah led with this simple declaration where he stated that he was "confessing the sins of the people of Israel, which we have sinned against you" (Neh. 1:6). Nehemiah began the heart of his prayer with confession.

This is the exact opposite of normal human nature. When I was young, and wanted something from my parents, I did not begin with a list of the things I had done wrong, because I figured bringing attention to my failures would sabotage my case. I would jump in to what I wanted while I had their attention. But Nehemiah knew that his prayer was about a lot more than merely getting something from God. It was about restoring a severed relationship.

The Israelites had been sent into exile and were still in partial bondage due to their disobedience to God. They had broken their side of the covenant by seeking other gods and ignoring God's commandments. Their acts of sin had damaged the relationship, not because their sins were what some today call "victimless crimes," but because they were sins against the relationship.

One danger of legalism is that it reduces obedience to God to a set of rules. But God never intended for us to follow a set of rules; He desired that we be in a relationship with Him. As far back as when Enoch walked with God (Gen. 5:24), when "the LORD used to speak to Moses face to face, as a man speaks to his friend" (Ex. 33:11), and up to the present, God does not want us to follow rules so much as to engage Him in fellowship. So while the Israelites in their rebellion broke a law, the bigger offense was that they broke the sacred trust that formed the core of their relationship with God.

David grasped this truth when he stated that "against you, you only, have I sinned and done what is evil in your sight" (Ps. 51:4). Wait! Didn't Bathsheba bear a child through David's adultery? Wasn't Uriah dead through David's betrayal? Yes, sin usually leaves a path of victims in its wake. But these victims were the byproduct of sin. The initial sin, the launching point that created this wreckage, was against God.

David continues in his understanding, stating that, because of his sin, God would be "justified in your words and blameless in your judgment" (Ps. 51:4). David knew that he deserved whatever punishment was given to him for his sin. He accepted God's sovereignty in the justice meted out.

During the Exile, the Israelites came to the same conclusion, that they were disobedient against God and deserved His judgment and the resulting punishment. Tragically, they placed more emphasis on the broken laws than on the severed relationship, and built a "law around the Law" to attempt to keep a safe barrier between them and disobedience. Their religious practices grew in legalism, which became a burden to the people.

But Nehemiah kept it personal. His first confession was to the Israelites' offenses against the Person of God. He would get into the particulars later. But first, Nehemiah wanted to convey his understanding to God that the Israelites had not just broken the laws of God. They had broken the personal bond between them and God.

## We Have All Sinned

Nehemiah's next words seem even more remarkable at first glance: "Even I and my father's house have sinned" (Neh. 1:6). Didn't the Exile start some 160 years earlier? Didn't the ongoing disobedience occur for hundreds of years prior to that? Nehemiah was not personally culpable for those actions. It would be like us today accepting responsibility for atrocities committed during the Crusades.

Nehemiah's statement is true on both counts. The easiest part to realize is that his father's house was complicit in sin. Of course they were! They were in Israel during the time Israel chose to worship other gods over Yahweh. If they were not actively participating in rebellion against God, they were either silently condoning it or not speaking up against it.

> **Nehemiah knew that his prayer was about restoring a severed relationship.**

Yet the Bible does not record of much of Nehemiah's life. Was he willful like Jacob or arrogant like Joseph when he was younger? The snapshot we have of Nehemiah focuses on the portion of his life dedicated to wall-building and religious reforms. One option is to take Nehemiah's word and accept that at some point he was guilty of sin against God.

Or we can look to the deeper truth presented here. Nehemiah was guilty because we all are guilty. Romans 3:23 was just as true two thousand years ago as it is today: "For all have sinned and fall short of the glory of God." He would have been familiar with the same concept as expressed by Isaiah: "All we like sheep have gone astray; we have turned—every one—to his own way" (Is. 53:6). Nehemiah was including himself in the universal population of mankind who have fallen short of God's standard and are deserving of God's judgment.

## Sin is Specific Deeds of Rebellion

After casting the net of sin over everyone, including himself and his family, Nehemiah confessed to specifics of the Israelites' sin. He first stated that "we have acted very corruptly against you" (Neh. 1:7). For something to be *corrupted* means for it to be perverted or go against its intended purpose. The corruption may seem to work for a season, but eventually things will go badly. The original intent of fuse boxes was to provide a release mechanism against excessive electrical current flowing through a house. A fuse contained a sliver of metal that was meant to be the weak point in the circuit. A current above the designed threshold would burn through the metal sliver and "blow" the fuse. With the circuit broken, power would be out until the blown fuse was replaced. People did not like this limitation on the amount of electrical power available, so they would replace the fuse with a copper penny. The fuse was no longer the weak point of the circuit, so the house would have unlimited power without the annoyance of a blown fuse.

Or so they thought. What was perceived as the weak and failing part of the electrical circuit was actually a safety feature. The fuse was designed to handle only a certain amount of current and fail when that amount was exceeded. The failure point of the fuse was set to be lower than the failure point of the rest of the wiring in the circuit. When the fuse blew, the rest of the wiring was safe. But if the limitation of the fuse was removed and replaced with a penny, the excessive current would eventually cause a failure elsewhere, likely the internal wiring of a house.

A humorous version of this scenario is seen in the movie *A Christmas Story*, where the fuse blows when the dad adds the leg lamp to the multitude of items connected to one outlet via octopus plugs. We see the brief flame, then the lights go out and he grabs a flashlight to go replace the fuse in the basement. Returning to the living room, he unplugs a couple items so that adding the lamp would stay within the limit set by the fuse. But if he had replaced the fuse with a penny, the flame we saw earlier would have been along the wiring inside the walls of the house, and the result would have been tragic rather than humorous.

The lesson learned is that, when something is corrupted by perverting its original purpose, the safety inherent in that purpose is also removed. Danger and destruction often follow quickly behind.

So when Nehemiah stated that they have acted corruptly towards God, he meant they had abandoned their original purpose for which they were created and replaced it with something less safe. It is easy to know that purpose because Nehemiah stated it: "[We] have not kept the commandments, the statutes, and the rules that you commanded your servant Moses" (Neh. 1:7).

God's covenant with Israel was established at Mount Sinai through Moses, confirmed later before entering the Promised Land, and confirmed again through Joshua after entering the Promised Land. The heart of this covenant is what we know as the Ten Commandments, which can be summarized as Israel forsaking all other gods to follow only Yahweh. This allegiance to God would be displayed in how they treated their fellow man. Israel failed badly on both counts.

It was not enough for Nehemiah to say that they were not perfect. He had to specify that their specific acts of rebellion against God were rejecting God's commands, statutes and rules. We must never downplay our sin against God. Rebellion against God is at the heart all of sin, regardless of the actual action or thought involved.

# The Miracle of Confession

Years ago I got an infection in my thumb while traveling. A minor nick near the thumbnail began to fester below the surface of my thumb, even after the initial skin wound had healed. The pressure built to where I was in significant discomfort returning home and severe pain the following day. I went to my doctor, who quickly diagnosed the problem. Numbing my thumb, he lanced the swollen section, immediately releasing pus and blood. After squeezing out every bit that was possible, he administered a local disinfectant and prescribed further medicine to heal the infection and prevent the problem from recurring. Even in the midst of the pain of the procedure, when it felt as if my thumb was being mashed by pliers, the immediate release of the infection-caused pressure brought relief, and I knew the thoroughness with which my doctor worked out the infected material would aid in the healing process.

We have a spiritual infection in our lives known as sin. It may fester below the surface for a season, but if it is untreated, the infection and resultant pain will keep growing. At some point, the pain becomes debilitating, to where we can no longer effectively function.

> ## Confession is the act by which we open our hearts to God for Him to work.

Confession is the miraculous procedure by which God lances the sin that infects our hearts. The actual procedure may seem gross and messy, but sin is gross and messy, regardless of how we may try to dress it up and give it a clean façade. God is our master Healer, ready to perform the procedure necessary to clean out all the gunk in our hearts. Confession is the act by which we open our hearts to God for Him to work.

Just as my doctor worked thoroughly to remove as much infected matter as possible, we must not take a shortcut with this procedure. We must allow God to dig down as deeply as possible to root out every bit of sinful junk. The process will be uncomfortable and humbling, but the result will be a release of inner pressure and the promise of healing.

Nehemiah knew the sinfulness of himself and his people. He knew that sin had separated them from God, and had caused their current situation. A full confession where he admitted rebellion against God was the necessary first step to invite God to again work in the lives of him and his people. It was through airing and cleaning out the negative that God would have room to operate in a more positive way.

# Prayer Building Block #5:
## Confession is the foundation for restoring our relationship with God.

## What is the sin in your life?

The specific list of individual sins does not matter at this stage, although they will be part of the process later. But the sin in your life is that you have offended God. You have rejected Him and His way to forge your own path, even if the steps are paved with legalistic zeal. You have chosen to disregard the relationship which God offers to you. Even if you have embraced God's offer of salvation, you are slighting the accompanying relationship. You have been corrupted by sin, sidelined from God's intended purpose for your life and at risk for danger and even disaster as long as you continue in sin.

Nehemiah knew that Israel's sin was against God, and that everyone was culpable in disobedience. The degree of disobedience did not matter, for God does not grade on a curve. Nehemiah fully admitted his role in the national rejection of God.

Since sin severs our relationship with God, confession of that sin is the step to restore our relationship with God. Nehemiah knew that, before he could speak to God about anything else, he must first restore that relationship. So it is with us today.

## How healthy is your relationship with God today?

Do you keep short accounts as Paul advised, continually taking sin to God and dealing with it quickly? Or are you ignoring your sin as it festers and grows, pretending it does not matter, just as you pretend that your relationship with God is not impacted by your rebellion?

Take the time that is needed to deal with your sin. All the great revivals began with an extensive time of confession, where people got serious about their sin and sought forgiveness and help from God. The ongoing miracle is that whenever we come to God in a spirit of confession, He is ready to forgive and receive us back into fellowship.

To release our sin to God and leave it with Him is a remarkably freeing process. We unburden ourselves while removing the barrier preventing deeper intimacy with God. As new sins try to erect new barriers to our fellowship, a practice of timely and true confession keeps the road smooth for our journey with God.

Come clean to God. Confession enables you to enjoy your relationship with God.

# Rebuilding

## Chapter 6

# Remembering God's Track Record

"No sport is less organized than Calvinball."
— *Hobbes, Calvin and Hobbes*[1]

Calvinball was the chaotic game invented by the central character in the *Calvin and Hobbes* comic strip that defied any attempt at order or consistent play. Pictures would show him using various balls and sports equipment that did not normally work together, such as a football, tennis racket, and croquet wickets. The game could never be played the same way twice. In fact, the only purpose to remember the rules was to ensure that prior rules could not be used again.

Remember. Such a simple yet powerful concept. Our memories tether us to our pasts, providing context and explanation for all we experience going forward in life. Each moment of life provides new lessons to be stored and recalled when needed. From something as basic as remembering to put toothpaste on a toothbrush to the lifesaving reminder to look before crossing a busy street, our ability to remember is engaged countless times each day.

What do we do when our memory is severed? How do we go forward without the foundation of the past? How do we rebuild our life if we no longer know our place or direction?

Movies like *The Vow* explore the concept of a young woman forgetting everything after an accident, including her newlywed husband. The husband has to court his wife again, in hopes that he can trigger and reactivate those memories in which she once loved him and married him.

Doctors say retrograde amnesia can occur after severe brain trauma, in which everything that occurred before the accident is forgotten. A psychological form of amnesia can also occur, where the mind blocks the memory of certain events because they are too traumatic to deal with at that point. In these circumstances, an inability to remember can be helpful to healing. But generally a loss of memory can be crippling, because we lose track of who we are.

It can also be traumatic when someone else you rely on does not remember what they should. The minor version is when someone forgets to bring home milk and bread from the store. The life-changing version is when someone forgets who you are, as the wife did in *The Vow*. The ancient Israelites feared God had forgotten them.

They had been exiled and partially returned to their homeland, only to remain under the control of other empires. They had a nominally rebuilt Temple, but Jerusalem remained defenseless to attack. They were oppressed and mocked by neighboring people. While they knew their punishment was a direct result of their sin, they needed to know that God remembered them and His past promises to them.

## Does God Need Help Remembering?

The simple answer is: No. As tempting as it may be to move on to the next section, some analysis must be done to determine why such a request would even be made. Nehemiah invokes God's memory in this portion of the prayer: "Remember the word that you commanded your servant Moses" (Neh. 1:8). A request made for someone to invoke a memory often embodies two goals: to seek consistency and to revisit past positive experiences.

People work best under a stable and reliable system of cause and effect. The best possible practice when raising children is to discipline consistently, where a similar action produces a similar encouragement or punishment. For a parent to be completely unpredictable builds stress and frustration in the child to where they refuse to follow any guidelines. This reliance on patterns continues as we become adults. We expect certain results from specific actions with a degree of consistency and reliability. This expected pattern is prevalent throughout all of life, from raising children to training dogs to living life.

Once the concept of patterns, or cause and effect, has been established, the goal is to seek out those actions within the pattern that produce the favorable response. Actions can potentially produce both positive and negative results. The remembering aspect of this process is to remember which actions produce positive results and which actions produce negative results. Part of learning the cause and effect cycle is understanding which actions produce the positive consequences, and to repeat the positive actions as frequently as possible.

Obviously, God does not need help remembering what He said earlier. What Nehemiah and the Israelites were seeking was their own understanding. They wanted to ensure that they recognized the cause and effect cycle established with the covenant earlier. Then they could properly follow God to receive the promised blessings rather than curses. Because, based on their history, they knew they could count on God being consistent and reliable in His actions.

## Remembering the Promise of Judgment

Children quickly develop selective memories, in which they remember the promise of goodies while forgetting the corresponding promise of punishment if they disobey. Nehemiah knew he was not dealing with a forgetful parent but with the omniscient God. He knows the reason for Israel's predicament. He knows they deserved God's judgment.

So, the first memory Nehemiah brought to God was the promised judgment: "If you are unfaithful, I will scatter you among the peoples" (Neh. 1:8). This is the conclusion to Deuteronomy 28, which presents a graphic description of this judgment, where exile is the least of the punishments, in Deuteronomy 28:15–68.

This judgment was precisely what happened to the Israelites. They suffered through the drought, poverty, invasions, and starvation that led to cannibalism before finally being taken prisoner and scattered to different empires. They came to this realization, while in exile, that they were the cause of their own demise.

What was the purpose of bringing up the obvious, especially to a God who not only knows everything but set forth the conditions? To communicate to that God that they understood fully now, that they *got it*. They knew that their current plight was the consequence of their actions, and that God is just in His judgments.

One aspect of our legal system that seems to be disappearing is the concept of remorse, in which the guilty party expresses sorrow over their actions. During sentencing, judges would often take the demeanor of the defendant into consideration when determining the sentence for the crime of which they had been declared guilty. If there was no remorse, the sentence would often be as severe as allowed under the law. If, on the other hand, the defendant seemed to show sincere regret for their actions, the sentence might be lessened since the defendant had already achieved the critical first step towards restoration, that of realizing that his actions were wrong.

Perhaps Israel was seeking a lessening of their punishment. However, the most important first step Israel could take, after confessing their sins as was discussed in the previous chapter, was to recognize the context of their disobedience and punishment within God's covenant program. Asking God to remember His own covenant may seem laughable, but what the Israelites were saying was that they remember the covenant and their inability to meet it. They remembered the contracts with God they agreed to at Sinai, at Gilgal, at Ebal, and at Shechem.

> **The Israelites knew that their current plight was the consequence of their actions, and that God was just in His judgments.**

They remembered that God set the rules to the covenant, and once agreed to, the rules would not change part-way through or when circumstances get tough. God is a God of integrity who always keeps His word. So, if His word involves judgment, that judgment must be meted out, even if after a long season of patiently waiting for a repentance that never came.

What Nehemiah was asking God to remember was that Israel now also remembered the rules and was ready to re-engage by living by the rules, including the consequences.

## Remembering the Promise of Deliverance

Then Nehemiah continued to the next step, which came with repentance: "[B]ut if you return to me and keep my commandments and do them, though your outcasts are in the uttermost parts of heaven, from there I will gather them and bring them to the place that I have chosen, to make my name dwell there" (Neh. 1:9). First of all, the prior section already covered God not needing to be told to remember something. The purpose was for the Israelites. They needed to tell God that they were ready to end their period of disobedience and reenter into covenant relationship with God. God made promises resulting in blessings for obedience and consequences for disobedience.

Since the promises of judgment referenced by Nehemiah are in Deuteronomy 28, Nehemiah also reached back to Deuteronomy for the promises of deliverance. His statement in Nehemiah 1:9 is a condensation of Deuteronomy 30:2–4. Having suffered under the consequences of breaking the covenant, the Israelites were seeking the blessings.

Were they really? Or were they just trying to avoid more suffering? This is where God's discernment of man's heart is crucial. We cannot know inner motives or true desires. We have to trust that what is communicated is honest. But God does know our hearts, and we can keep nothing hidden from Him. We cannot fool God with false remorse.

Nehemiah did not explicitly make the case at this point for genuine repentance. He hoped that his actions and attitude, especially during the last months, showed that he was contrite over present and past sins. He wanted God to know that he was ready to cast aside all rebellion to enter into renewed relationship.

## Remembering Past Acts of Redemption

God's past record of redeeming His people is declared next: "They are your servants and your people, whom you have redeemed by your great power and by your strong hand" (Neh. 1:10). The Israelites understood that their very existence as a nation was due to God pulling them out of pagan cultures. First, Abraham was chosen from his people and led to the Promised Land. Later, his grandson Jacob was brought back from his pagan family to inhabit that same land.

The central event in Israelite life, the anniversary of which began their year, was God miraculously delivering them from slavery in Egypt. God redeemed them from bondage using the blood of the Passover lamb. Pharaoh withstood the prior plagues that devastated Egypt, but after a night of widespread death during which the Israelites were spared, he finally relented and allowed them to leave. Even when Pharaoh changed his mind again and pursued the Israelites, God intervened to bring Israel to freedom while defeating Egypt.

Mere escape was not sufficient. God provided for Israel as they shook off sin in the wilderness and took the initial steps to establish a nation. God fought for Israel as they invaded and conquered the Promised Land. God established a new home in the land He had promised to their forefathers, defeating their enemies and allowing them peace and prosperity.

Whenever the Hebrews looked at examples of God's past provision in their lives, the deliverance from Egypt was the central reminder. It was during this time that God's covenant expanded from being personal with a family to being national with the people of Israel. The Passover was so significant in the lives of the Israelites that its practice remained one of their primary religious celebrations some 1,400 years later during the life of Jesus.

There can be no doubt that their current situation paled in comparison to what God had done in the past. While they were allowed to return to Israel, they were still under the control of the Persian Empire. They had no means to defend themselves from neighboring peoples. They had no protection since the city walls were torn down. No freedom, no peace, no prosperity.

The natural response was for Nehemiah to reach back to a time when God delivered and provided for His people. The Israelites were not perfect then; they still rebelled. But they quickly repented and came back to God. God always forgave them and continued in relationship. Nehemiah's goal was that, having seen the repentance of him and his people, God would take note of the past acts of redemption and work in a similar fashion to bring His people to a new place of peace and prosperity through a renewal of their covenant relationship.

## The Remembering is for Us

The whole purpose of recording something is to have it as a source of reference at a later time. When God's word was initially recorded, the people of Israel could refer back to it and see how God worked in the past. The Bible also records how the next generation often grew up, forgetting what God had done and turning instead to other gods. They did not look at God's track record but were blinded by the allure of others.

The recording of God's work was not just for Israel; it was for all of mankind. It was for us, today, when our technological advances make us arrogant and boastful, believing that we can accomplish anything in this world. Modern faithless man pushes even the concept of an active God into the realm of superstition, haughtily looking down on anyone who "believes." We dispense with ancient myths and seek to carve out our own way.

Faithless man explains miracles through science, or failing that, pseudoscience. Anything to reject the notion of an active God will suffice, regardless how shaky the foundation. The past must be explained differently, without

> **The recording of God's work was not just for Israel, it was for all of mankind.**

God, so that modern man can bravely go forward without allegiance to or even acknowledgement of any higher power.

We must reject the naysayers, the deniers of God's presence and power. Nehemiah recognized the active work of God in the past as a hope for the presence of God in the future. We need to claim Israel's history as our own. While God's methods of working may have changed, that does not alter the power or reality of God's working.

The tendency of man throughout history has been doubt as justification for willfulness. Nehemiah knew that weakness, and modern advances intensify the pull from faith to unbelief. It is through an effective and honest reading of history, both in the Bible and in our own lives, that we build our faith. When we remember what God has done, we are positioned to look forward to what God will do.

# Prayer Building Block #6:
## Remembering what God has done in the past gives us confidence for what God will do in the future.

## What is the history of God in your life?

As you look back and walk through your life's major events, can you detect the handiwork of God? Perhaps the friendship established when you were otherwise alone. Maybe the friendship parting ways just prior to that person entering into destructive patterns. It could have been God sustaining you through difficult, even horrific experiences, and allowing you to maintain hope.

By this stage of Old Testament history, Nehemiah could easily trace the hand of God working in the people of Israel, with much of it recorded. He did not have to grasp or guess at evidence of God's presence. God had announced His actions through His spokesmen as they were being done.

But our cynical and faithless age today denies the work of God, past or present. It is too easy to be caught up in that lie and believe that God does not care about your plight or your future. Do not succumb to the temptation to view the past through the filters of doubt that erase God's work in your life.

God is active in all our lives, arranging and using people and events in ways we cannot begin to comprehend, much less figure out. We will never know all that we avoided or all the different alternatives that could have occurred in our lives. Lacking an authoritative scribe, we will need to import the track record of the Israelites for our own, believing that the God who was at work thousands of years ago is still active, still caring, still present.

## Faith is strengthened through experience.

In our human experience, we stand at the threshold between past and future, the present flipping by like pages in a book. Each present moment quickly becomes part of an ever-growing past, building up a volume of experience and memories. Do not let the doubters steal your present and rewrite your past. Understand how God is at work, so that what is remembered is how God was active in the situations.

As you understand your life in the context of God's presence, His working will begin to pop out, like 3D illustrations in a children's book, with each page revealing new evidence as it is opened and examined. Then the book of your life becomes a testimony to the power of God working in your life.

Remembering what God has done in your past builds the faith to walk with God in your future.

# Rebuilding

# Chapter 7

# Letting God Define Success

"Young man, the secret of my success is that at an early age I
discovered I was not God."
– *Oliver Wendell Holmes, Jr.* [1]

When I was younger, I could be an ungrateful brat. One Christmas, my brother and I wanted *The Men from U.N.C.L.E* BB guns. I do not remember if they were out of stock, my parents could not afford them, or that they were just impractical for boys our age, but when we opened our presents Christmas morning, we found Daisy BB Guns instead of what we had wanted. We moped and complained until my dad suggested he take everything away. Faced with the potential loss of our Christmas haul, we quickly changed our tune. But we initially resented these gifts because they were not what we wanted.

Looking back, I am amazed that my parents ever gave me another gift. The Daisy rifle was fine quality, and I shot it for many years. Yet I had gotten so specific in my desires that simply a BB gun was not sufficient. It had to have a specific logo from a specific television program. Anything else was second best, to be accepted only as a substitute for what I really wanted. I, as a child, had placed myself in the position of knowing what was better for me than my own parents.

Getting what we want is one basic definition of success. We can be picky and specific, like I had been with my BB gun choice, or we can be more general. Either way, we are seeking our own way and setting expectations, and then defining our success in terms of how close we are to achieving or acquiring our goal.

The Israelites had specific goals in mind, too, when they sought God's favor. They wanted a free land where they were not oppressed by the people around them. They wanted a rebuilt Temple, matching the glory and opulence of Solomon's Temple, where they could resume the sacrifices central to their worship of God. They wanted an intact capital where they could defend themselves from attack. They also wanted a restored relationship with God as the foundation for getting all the other things they wanted.

This is where it gets tricky. Did Israel want the relationship with God as a means to get all the other things they wanted, or was the relationship with God their final goal, with anything else as blessings overflowing in their lives?

# God and Hidden Agendas

It can be easy for people to say they want God, when all they really want is to use God to get what they truly want. People do that all the time in relationships. They feign interest in one thing or person as a means to get to their true hidden goal. If played skillfully, the used person has no knowledge that they were simply a tool used in pursuit of a goal. They might catch on after the fact when they were discarded, but by then their usefulness is done, so it does not matter to the person who took advantage of them.

A brief review of Israel's history suggests they might have been using God to get what they want, rather than seeking fellowship with God as their primary goal. In the book of Judges, each new generation had to relearn trusting God alone instead of including the gods from the people around them. The standard excuse for disobedience was to cloak themselves in fake spirituality. Later, King Saul, when challenged about his disobedience in bringing back flocks and herds from an enemy instead of killing them, protested that he wanted to bring back a sacrifice for God. When Israel split into two kingdoms, the Northern Kingdom built an altar at Dan so the people did not have to travel to Jerusalem and be potentially pulled back into Temple worship. Throughout their history, Israel acted no better than the surrounding pagans in that they tried to placate God through worship to get what they wanted.

But a further reading of the Old Testament shows that God was not fooled by faux spirituality. Saul was removed as king for his acts of disobedience. Israel came under repeated attack from outside enemies for their refusal to forsake other gods and worship God alone, a pattern that culminated in the destruction of the Temple and Jerusalem. They were given the opportunity to cool their heels

> It can be easy for people to say they want God, when all they really want is to use God to get what they truly want.

in exile for seventy years while they pondered the error of their ways.

God, being omniscient, cannot be fooled by fake spirituality. For us to attempt to do so is as foolish as a two-year-old who thinks he is hiding from us because his hands are covering his eyes and he cannot see us. We cannot hide our agendas from God. We cannot use pagan practices or rites to appease God while lacking transformation in our hearts. The only way to success with God is to be fully honest and transparent in our goals.

## Micromanaging God

I have suffered under a few micromanagers in my life, and it became tiresome very quickly. They were not content to assign me a task, or to even point me in a beneficial direction. No, they immersed themselves in every step of the process, reducing me from a thinking person to an extension of themselves. Some of these managers were actually competent at the work. Frustration elevated to anger when the micromanager had been long removed from a job I knew better, but they still insisted on dictating every single step of an assigned task. I sought ways to hide from them because I knew that no progress could be made while they were present.

Micromanaging killed my morale because, in the end, I knew the manager did not trust me to do the job properly. It may have been an obsessive need for control on his part, but the impact was the same. I was not merely asked to do something, but told in meticulous detail how I had to do it, with no flexibility or freedom to pick a better option.

If I was that frustrated with a meddling manager, imagine how God feels when we do not just petition Him for something, but instruct Him as to how to do His job. He's been at it longer than us, and He knows a bit more than us. Yet we still presume to lecture God on the best outcome of our request or situation.

It sounds absurd when placed in those terms, but that is how we often approach God. We are not content to seek God's intervention; we must instruct God as to the particulars of His intervening. Perhaps we want a certain timing, or want God to work in a way that removes our pain without requiring much sacrifice on our part. The result is that we have assumed the position of God's taskmaster, and that is never a good place to be.

Then, when God rightfully and wisely ignores our detailed instructions and works His will, we interpret the different results as a negative response from God, or even indifference from God. We lose faith because we had predicated God's faithfulness on His ability to achieve the exact outcome that we desired. We fail to see God at work because we do not see God working in the precise manner we dictated to Him. Our attempts to micromanage God have become a stumbling block to our faith.

## Letting God be God

Nehemiah knew that God was sovereign over everything and did not need to be instructed. He presented his request to God, but gave God the latitude to determine the best manner in which to work. He presented his plea very simply at the end of his prayer: "[G]ive success to your servant today, and grant him mercy in the sight of this man" (Neh. 1:11).

What Nehemiah does do is set parameters in which he hopes to see God work. First, Nehemiah seeks success *today*. This may have been an actual twenty-four hour day, or it may have been a current time period. Either way, Nehemiah is looking to God in the present time and not some unspecified future time. There is a sense of urgency to the request.

Next, Nehemiah is seeking God's mercy in action. It may not have been given directly from God, but God would definitely be involved. How that mercy would happen was in God's hands, but was a very specific tone or quality desired in the situation. Seeking mercy is a substantially different request than seeking vengeance on one's enemies, or seeking to restore the greatness Israel had experienced under kings David and Solomon.

Finally, Nehemiah specifies the person in whom he needs God to work. "This man" was the king of Persia, which Nehemiah identifies in his closing statement, "Now I was cupbearer to the king" (Neh. 1:11). Nehemiah's position of service placed him in regular proximity to the very man with the power to enact what needed to happen. God could have used anyone, but had placed Nehemiah in the position of trust regarding the most powerful man in the empire.

This is where Nehemiah's trusting God in the details is distinct from fatalism. A fatalist may back away from any emotional involvement or commitment to a given situation, simply declaring that God will work when and how He chooses to work. While technically true, this attitude requires no faith, because we are not expecting God to work and are not disappointed when nothing happens.

But Nehemiah expects God to work, and even draws broad parameters in which he hopes to see God work. True faith is active and hopeful, always looking to see God in action. It must be specific enough to know where to look to see God in action yet broad enough to give God the latitude to be God and let Him work His will in the situation.

## Expecting God to Work

True active faith requires both giving God the space to work while believing that God will indeed work. Years ago, I heard a pastor from Uganda speak of the amazing growth of the church in their city. The first week, the small building was overflowing. So, during the week, they opened the back wall and expanded the building to accommodate more people. The following Sunday, they were overflowing again. So they expanded the building more the next week, only to be overflowing yet again. This continued each week for months, until they had grown from beginning the church to 30,000 people coming on Sunday.

Many of these people had walked for hours to attend the service. Many were poor, and lacking proper footwear to make the trek or ample food and water for a day-long outing consisting of

> [Faith] must be specific enough to know where to look to see God in action yet broad enough to give God the latitude to be God and let Him work.

walking to church and back home. They could have been lacking proper medical care, or funds to send their children to school. The needs of the people flooding into the church were overwhelming, not to mention the sheer logistics of managing such large numbers so quickly.

But the pastor and leaders did not turn people away, nor did they throw their hands in the air in resignation, accepting whatever happened. They sought God in prayer, and expected God to work in this astounding growth and appalling level of need. The summary of their prayer, as told to us by the pastor, was, "Lord, if you don't show up, we're toast!"[2]

They knew the needs of the people, both spiritual and material. They knew God had brought the people to their church. They would minister to the people as best they could, but knew their efforts would be inadequate. So they beseeched God for help. They knew that, without God, failure would be a certainty. God was their only hope for success in this endeavor. There was no Plan B.

We need to maintain the proper balance in our faith. On one extreme, we are micromanaging God, instructing Him on how to fulfill our wishes. On the other extreme, we drop into passivity or fatalism, not caring what God does or when He does it, while presenting a façade of faith. The best ground to stand on is in the middle, where we expectantly look for God to work yet leave the details in His hands.

# There is no Plan B

Nehemiah could pray with faith because he knew his success depended on God showing up in the situation. When God was his Plan A, there was no Plan B. There was no means in which Nehemiah could take steps to meet the need he saw in Jerusalem. He had to place his full trust in God for there to be success.

Using that trust as a foundation, Nehemiah could then place the method of meeting the need in God's hands. He allowed God to determine how to work in the situation. Nehemiah set parameters for two purposes. First, these parameters would clarify the need so that Nehemiah fully understood what was needed. Second, setting parameters provides a place to look to see God working. If we are not specific in our requests, we have no idea whether or not God answered us. We are establishing a framework in which to see God work.

Dependence does not mean fatalism or apathy. We can eagerly await God while fully relying on God. Nehemiah knew this tension and expressed it in his prayers, seeking God's intervention *today*. Nehemiah fully trusted that, in God's perfect timing, one day *today* would arrive and God would work. Nehemiah's faith was a trusting, expectant faith, not one of apathy or indifference.

This attitude can be summarized as *expectant surrender*. On one hand, we are expectant. We assume that God will be active and working, to the point that we draw parameters around our situation to look in a specific area for God to act in our situation. But we are also in an attitude of surrender, in which we let God determine how and when He will work. We keep all possibilities open, even outside our expectant parameters, because we are letting God define success in our situation. We must continually balance these two attitudes when we petition God in prayer.

In the situation of the Ugandan church, God did show up. People came to Christ. Lives were transformed. The entire community was blessed. God was doing a mighty work through the church that was dependent on Him.[3]

# Prayer Building Block #7:
## Expect God to work in your life but do not tell Him how.
## There is no Plan B.

## When you pray, are you wishful or expectant?

Are you treating your petition to God with no more seriousness or faithfulness in His work than if you made a wish while tossing coins in a fountain? Or do you expect God to be faithful and act on your behalf?

Likewise, when you seek something from God, are you seeking His will in your situation, or are you handing God a set of instructions to follow? Has your faith in God been diminished because He is not operating per your direction and answering according to your preferences?

Or have you given up relying on God altogether? You may pray to God, and seek His favor, but you plan and live your life to exist without God's intervention. Even those efforts done on behalf of God are designed to succeed within your known abilities and resources. God may choose to bless what you are doing, but you can accomplish what you set out without God even being present.

Nehemiah knew his task was futile without God's intervention and active involvement. Nehemiah did not even know when God would work. While plans were made and parameters were set, Nehemiah trusted God above his own sensibilities. He knew *where* God needed to work, but he was not going to dictate *how* God was going to work. Nehemiah needed God for success to happen. There was no Plan B.

## Take a look at your life and your various situations.

Is there a place where God needs to work that you have not entrusted to God? Perhaps you set too-specific directions, and only defined success as meeting those criteria. Perhaps you gave up looking for God to work in that area and made your own efforts, only to flounder and make no progress. Perhaps you deemed the matter too small, too hopeless, too *whatever* for God to even bother.

Pray the prayer of Nehemiah over that area. Develop a sense of urgency, where you expect God to arrive. Build some parameters to understand where to look for God to work, but leave all the details, including the timing, in His hands. Let God define success for your situation, but know that He will be active. Above all, do not become discouraged and take matters into your own hands, pushing God out of the picture.

When it comes to faithfully expecting God to work, there is no Plan B.

Rebuilding

# Chapter 8

# Opportunistic Prayer

"There is not in the world a kind of life more sweet and delightful,
than that of a continual conversation with God."
– *Brother Lawrence*[1]

One of the cliché television scenes in a doctor's office had the patient sitting on the examining table. The doctor would take a small white mallet with a tapered end and firmly tap the patient's knee. The patient's knee would reflexively shoot out in a kicking motion, and the doctor would say, "Well, your reflexes are fine."

That is more than a cliché. There actually is a spot on your knee where, if you strike it just right, causes an involuntary response that jerks your leg out. When growing up, my friends and I would try to hit the same spot to get the reaction. Although we missed most of the time, we used it as an excuse to kick out at the other person. But when the right spot was struck, the sensation was odd, because your leg jerked up independent of your thinking about it or choosing to take any action.

Prayer can be looked at in the same way. It can be either an automatic reflexive response to outward stimuli, or it can be a forced response that mimics the effortless prayers of others, yet is artificially contrived without any of the sensation. Some people seem to naturally flow into prayer, while others need to be reminded that prayer is even an option. How can we move from prayers only by effort to prayer as a natural reflexive response? A peek at Nehemiah's prayers gives us some insight into the heart of a man who was in the habit to "pray without ceasing" (1 Thess. 5:17).

# Spontaneous Prayer

When people can relax and plan their day, they can incorporate all the things they would like to do. It is easy to include prayer and spending time with God as a desired part of a well-conceived day. However, when people are under stress or pressure, their response will be automatic. Their reply will be more instinctive rather than thought out or developed. Our reflexes will overshadow our intentions.

Nehemiah provides an excellent glimpse into his heart in the opening verses of Nehemiah chapter two when he offered an example of a spontaneous prayer perhaps unmatched in the entire Old Testament. He had already prayed (or been praying) his heart to God as described in chapter one.

Then one day, when Nehemiah was attending to the king, the king noticed something different in Nehemiah and asked, "Why is your face sad, seeing you are not sick? This is nothing but sadness of the heart" (Neh. 2:2).

Nehemiah was afraid but proceeded to reply to the king: "Let the king live forever! Why should not my face be sad when the city, the place of my fathers' graves, lies in ruins, and its gates have been destroyed by fire?" (Neh. 2:3). Even while responding to the king's concern, Nehemiah remained respectful and maintained his position as servant and not equal, even while responding honestly and boldly.

The king's response was simple and direct: "What are you requesting?" (Neh. 2:4). The opportunity had been presented to Nehemiah.

What happened next comes so quickly as to be easily overlooked. In fact, most people focus on Nehemiah's thorough response, which had been obviously thought out. Nehemiah requested a leave of duty, safe transportation, supplies to rebuild the Jerusalem city walls and gates, and a letter from the king authorizing these actions and granting Nehemiah the authority to complete the task. A textbook case of planning ahead and waiting for the right time to execute the plan. But what is most significant is what occurred prior to the prepared response: "So I prayed to the God of heaven" (Neh. 2:4). Nehemiah's first response, in perhaps the most critical situation in his life, was to pray.

## Prayer as First Response

We might have the best intentions to pray. We might have a deep desire to spend time with God. But if prayer does not come naturally to us, it will not come when we are under duress. Our first response will be the instinctive one, as the first place to turn will be to where we had been relying upon up to that point.

Nehemiah demonstrated that his prayer in Nehemiah chapter one had not been a one-time event but an ongoing pattern. Prayer had been a natural response throughout his life, so it was the natural response during a critical time. Scripture does not even record the actual words of his prayer. The comment is wedged into Nehemiah's conversation with the king. It was as if prayer was such a normal occurrence that the words were not necessary to include in his memoirs.

That is precisely the point. Prayer was such a normal occurrence with Nehemiah that this response could almost be assumed. Yet this is the most obvious account of spontaneous prayer in the Bible. Prayer would be

> **Prayer had been a natural response throughout his life, so it was the natural response during a critical time.**

Nehemiah's first response because it had become his natural response in all situations.

Prayer is not the normal natural response for humans, especially in our current state. Our natural, sinful response is to determine what we can accomplish on our own. If we have exhausted our own means, we might seek help from others, and possibly even God. But this would be after our own efforts have failed. We need to reprogram ourselves from being self-reliant to being God-reliant.

## Building a Natural Response

When I coached baseball for youths, we began every practice with ground ball drills. While different specialty skills would be required for specific positions, every player needed to be skilled at fielding ground balls.

So, to begin every practice, we formed the players into two lines, with one line facing the other line.

A player on one side would throw a grounder to the opposite player and move to the back of the line. We monitored each player's stance, how they positioned their glove, how they positioned their other hand, how they fielded the ball, and how quickly they released the ball. We continually made adjustments and corrected players. There was no room for sloppiness. A player could field five grounders cleanly, but if he got lazy on the next grounder, we called him on it. We were patient with players developing their skills, but there was no tolerance for sloppy fundamentals.

The reason we were so tough on grounder drills was because we wanted to ingrain proper fielding technique into our players so they would not have to even think about the correct way to field a ground ball during a game. If a player was sloppy or careless during practice, he might be sloppy or careless during a game and commit costly errors. We wanted to build proper fielding technique into our players as their natural response, so they would automatically respond with the proper technique during the pressure of a game. The response practiced was likely to be the one exhibited when it mattered.

Drilling players on fundamentals may work regarding sports and muscle memory, but can we accomplish the same result with our ongoing relationship with God and connecting through prayer? Can such a rote practice build our prayer life from incidental to natural, where prayer becomes our natural first response and not a last resort?

First of all, many Christian leaders throughout history have regarded certain Christian practices, such as Bible reading, fasting, and prayer, as *spiritual disciplines*. The very term suggests that effort is put into intentionally building these practices into our lives. We are not to wait until they become convenient, but to work at making them happen. That might be feasible for the other practices, but prayer? Can spending time with God be defined as a task that we practice?

Our physical, carnal selves will easily forget about God during the busyness of the day's activities. We can put our spiritual selves on the back burner to be summoned if needed but ignored until that time. Our innate self-reliance can default to working things out on our own. Yes, we need to practice being with God. Fortunately for us, someone in the past made a life's work out of this very practice, and many of his thoughts on the subject have been captured and saved for our benefit.

## Practicing God's Presence

*The Practice of the Presence of God* by Brother Lawrence is a classic work that he would likely be embarrassed to know existed. He became a convert as an adult, after spending time as a soldier. He did not even think himself worthy to become a monk, so he remained a lay brother, limiting himself to working in the kitchen and garden. The reason the book even exists is because of a series of conversations and letters between Brother Lawrence and Joseph de Beaufort. The purpose of this interaction? To learn the "secrets" of Brother Lawrence's spirituality. Here are some selected quotes, along with how they can help us overcome our inherent self-centeredness and focus on God:

- "That we should establish ourselves in a sense of God's presence, by continually conversing with him" (First Conversation).[2] This is the goal of 1 Thessalonians 5:17, which instructs us to "pray without ceasing." This does not mean we need to be on our knees at all times, but that we can converse with God in whatever we are doing. Brother Lawrence found he could converse with God just as easily while peeling potatoes as when on his knees. We can adopt the same attitude and see our entire day as an opportunity to converse with God, instead of reserving it for special "prayer times."

- "That we ought to act with God in the greatest simplicity, speaking to Him frankly and plainly" (Second Conversation).[3] Too many people resist praying because they cannot speak in a high or formal "prayer language." This is an unnecessary barrier. God wants honesty and simplicity in our prayers. My wife prays very effectively by simply telling God what is on her heart. The Psalmists expressed all kinds of emotions when writing down their prayers. Part of ongoing conversing with God is that we come to Him as we are, and speak as we normally speak.

- "That our sanctification did not depend upon changing our works, but in doing that for God's sake which we commonly do for our own" (Fourth Conversation).[4] This embodies the concept of daily surrender to God. We do not need to limit our prayer time to church services or "church work." All our work is ordained by God and is made holy by His presence in our lives. Once we discard the old notion of sacred and secular, every activity of every day becomes worship and a celebration of all God has given. Then we naturally converse with God because we are performing that activity to the glory of God.

- "I drove away from my mind everything that was capable of interrupting my thought of God" (First Letter).[5] Distractions. We can all begin our day with the best of intentions, but urgent or distracting matters can derail our minds and leave us at the end of the day, wondering where we went and how we got there. Brother Lawrence recognized the same power of interruptions, and sought to push them out of his mind once they entered. We cannot stop distractions from knocking at our door, and we need discernment to determine if a distraction is really a divine appointment. But the distractions which pull us from the presence of God must be shown the door and banished from our minds.

> Part of ongoing conversing with God is that we come to Him as we are, and speak as we normally speak.

- "One way to re-collect the mind easily in the time of prayer, and preserve it more in tranquility, is not to let it wander too far at other times" (Eighth Letter).[6] Here, Brother Lawrence addresses the issue of our minds wandering during prayer, a common problem both then and now. His solution is to stay more focused on God at *all* times, not just during times of prayer. We cannot compartmentalize our lives. It is impossible to live a portion of our lives separate from God and then be able to draw close to God when desired. We are encouraged to keep our minds on God at all times, so that our focus is more present during times of devoted prayer.

## Spiritual Calisthenics

The whole book is a treasure worth reading and meditating through, but I have gleaned five principles that can help us build a God-centered life that helps to produce prayer as the first and natural response:

1) We should establish a practice of continually conversing with God.
2) We need to speak with God naturally and simply, using our normal language.
3) We need see every activity as holy and in God's presence, being done for His glory.
4) We need to drive away all distractions which take us from the presence of God.
5) We need to always stay mindful of God and not reserve Him for special times.

Following these principles can help us build the presence God into our normal, daily lives. Once we are comfortable with conversing with God throughout the day and during our various activities, it will become natural to turn to God in times of stress as our first response. It is a practice, to be considered as a discipline, because we are going against our carnal natures that pursue self-reliance independent of God. We seek to reprogram ourselves, our thought life, and our reflexive responses.

Nehemiah had already developed this pattern and lifestyle of prayer, so when the king requests a response, Nehemiah quickly turned to God, likely silently, before giving his response. This had become so normal that it was his reflexive response. Nehemiah did not need to remind himself to pray; he naturally turned to the God with whom he was already in regular conversation.

We can build the same lifestyle of prayer and be in regular conversation with God, so that we naturally turn to God in times of stress or urgency. We even have the advantage of the indwelling Holy Spirit to prompt us. But we must build this into our lives.

# Prayer Building Block #8:
## Make conversing with God part of your daily life.

## How much time do you spend with God during the day?

Do you talk to God throughout the day, or do you put your interaction with God on the shelf with your Bible after devotions? How much do you consider every activity as holy to God? Or are your activities categorized as either "with God" or "on your own"?

The only way to be able to call on God for help when under stress is to develop the practice of conversing with God at all times, especially times that are not urgent. If you follow the five steps outlined above, not as a recipe, but as a lifestyle, you will develop and deepen your relationship with God. The more you *practice* the presence of God in your life, the more you will desire to *know* the presence of God in your life.

Then, when tough times come, you will naturally turn to God, because you have been walking alongside God all along. What was once practiced has become natural and normal. You instinctively turn to God because you have been enjoying the fellowship of His presence up to this point.

## Nehemiah knew he could not succeed without God's help.

So, at the crucial point in his conversation with the king, Nehemiah turned to God for help before responding to the king: the same God that Nehemiah always turned to in times of stress. The same God that Nehemiah had been intensely praying to for months. The same God that Nehemiah prayed to on a continual basis.

Talk to God. Continually.

## Chapter 9

# Blending Prayer and Action

"Planners may be rightfully concerned about Rambo-type behavior
in management—'fire-fire-fire' in every direction, with no aiming.
But managers must be equally wary of planning behavior
that amounts to 'ready, aim. Aim.'"
– *Henry Mintzberg*[1]

Business consultants warn against two opposing extremes of
behavior. On one side, there is the mindless activity, characterized by acting
or reacting without thinking or analysis. Jim Collins referenced this mindset
as part of his "Doom Loop" in *Good to Great*, in which he described how
businesses would take action without realizing the root problem, only to make
the problem worse.[2] On the other side are the over-analysts, who spend so
much time thinking about an issue and researching every possible related
matter that nothing ever gets accomplished. Both extremes are shown as much
worse than a blended alternative between the two extremes.

Christians can fall into two similar extremes. On one side there are
the activists, who engage in frenzied activity, hoping that some of it is
beneficial to God's kingdom. There is no time for meditation because they
feel compelled to *do* things for God. On the other side are the contemplative
believers who view themselves as more spiritual. They are content to wait on
God and take no action until receiving clear confirmation from God to
proceed. In fact, they may refuse to act at all and depend on God miraculously
intervening in their situation. Neither extreme reflects an active and healthy
relationship with God.

Nehemiah knew the importance of prayer—he saturated his life in prayer and went to God for all matters. But Nehemiah did not wait for God to work supernatural miracles. Nehemiah held the ideal middle ground, blending prayer and action in a manner that showed both his dependence on God and his personal responsibility to *work* with God.

# Having a Tentative Plan

In the previous chapter, we looked at Nehemiah's heart for spontaneous prayer, in which he prayed in the midst of a discussion with the king in Nehemiah chapter two. But now, we need to take a close look at Nehemiah's answer after he prayed: "If it pleases the king, and if your servant has found favor in your sight, that you send me to Judah, to the city of my fathers' graves, that I may rebuild it" (Neh. 2:5).

Subsequent verses describe in detail how Nehemiah requested official letters through which to obtain the materials and safety needed to finish the project. This was a complete, thought-out answer given to hopefully guarantee success.

Nehemiah had been praying about this matter for three months, so he also had plenty of time to think about what needed to be done, as well as his potential role in the solution. He knew that success rested entirely in the hands of God, but when God presented the opportunity through the king's favorable attitude, Nehemiah was ready with a tentative plan. If God wanted to modify the plan in any manner, Nehemiah would accept the result as part of an attitude of surrender to God. But Nehemiah would have a plan ready that could be used.

We see the blending of prayer and action uniting perfectly in this discourse. Nehemiah prayed continually, as seen in Nehemiah chapter one, to submit to God and set his heart right before God. The goal of his prayer was to seek success as God defined it, likely connected to receiving favor from the king, since the king controlled Nehemiah's life at this stage. Then, once God had supplied the opportunity before the king, Nehemiah prayed prior to giving his response. We do not know the words of the prayer, but given the context, it was likely to be a prayer for wisdom in words used and mercy in the king granting a favorable answer to Nehemiah's request.

The action is shown by Nehemiah's preparation before the discourse ever took place. Nehemiah did not know when he would receive an opportunity with the king, so he had to be prepared at any time. The opportunity was not likely to repeat itself, so he had to have his best answer ready. The preparation showed that Nehemiah cared enough about this issue to make the wisest plans he could to give his project the best plan of success.

Someone who was more of an activist might have jumped ahead of God's timing and beseeched the king sooner. This would probably have resulted in a negative response, and if the king were badgered with follow-up requests, a possible removal of that activist from his position of closeness to the king. Then any opportunity for the king's help would be lost forever. Someone relying only on prayer might have tried to garner the plans from God mid-conversation, instead of preparing for the opportunity. God might have blessed that person in spite of their unpreparedness, but that would be solely up to God's grace. Too many Christian ministries have foundered because the leaders were expecting God to cover for their lack of planning, rather than using their own God-given intellects to better prepare and manage the ministry. Nehemiah merged the ideal combination of personal preparation and reliance on God in this situation.

> Nehemiah understood that seeking God through prayer was a necessary prelude to his subsequent response and action.

## Pray, Then Act

Nehemiah chapter four describes great progress being made on rebuilding the wall. Nehemiah has scouted the city, apportioned the work to the various groups of people, and successfully begun the task. Those opposed to this effort were not pleased, and sought to distract those involved. They were willing to resort to violence to stop the effort: "And they all plotted together to come and fight against Jerusalem and to cause confusion in it" (Neh. 4:8).

Since Nehemiah had fended off their initial ridicule, the opponents threatened physical violence. This threat could not be taken lightly, and could potentially result in everyone abandoning the project. It is one thing to continue working under ridicule; it is quite another to persist under threat of attack. How would the people react to this new threat? How should Nehemiah respond to this higher threat of attack?

Nehemiah replied with a classic combination of prayer and action: "And we prayed to our God and set a guard as a protection against them day and night" (Neh. 4:9). Nehemiah prayed first, as he did in any and all situations. He then took concrete action to guard and defend against any potential attack. The call to both God and arms is reminiscent of Oliver Cromwell's call to "pray to God and keep your powder dry."[3] The medieval monks practiced the motto *ora et labora*, translated as "pray and work," which embodied the concept practiced by Nehemiah.[4]

Nehemiah repeated this concept in Nehemiah 4:14–15 when, in response to yet another threat from their opponents, he encouraged Israel to remember God and fight for their brothers. Not only did Nehemiah see prayer as a normal response to any crisis or difficulty, but he understood that seeking God through prayer was a necessary prelude to his subsequent response and action.

## Who is Responsible for What?

When we examine Nehemiah's practice of blending prayer and action, we see a perfect representation of the respective roles of God and man. Nehemiah did not attempt to usurp God, and he also did not abdicate his responsibilities and expect God to miraculously intervene to cover up the lack of effort. The working out of God's will seems to follow along this blended pattern.

First and foremost, God is responsible for any and all success of endeavors in His kingdom work. He will work out His perfect timing, and He will soften or change hearts to achieve His will. In fact, He does not require our help at all, and can intervene miraculously, even transcending natural laws if needed. God is able to accomplish His will entirely on His own.

However, God has chosen to involve us in His work. While able to work miraculously, He has chosen to use the Church as His primary instrument for accomplishing His will during this age. This means that we are more than spectators to God's handiwork. We often have specific actions to take to serve God and see His kingdom advance.

But before we take our marching orders and run, we need to remember that God will remain active even as He involves us in His work.

Involving us does not mean that God hands off the task, washes His hands of all responsibility, and then passively waits to see whether we succeed or fail. Yet much Christian work is done with the implied opinion that all responsibility lies on them to achieve God's work, with God as only a passive spectator.

When God involves us in His work, He is inviting us into partnership with Him. We need to slow down and recognize how incredible an opportunity we have: *the Lord of the Universe desires that we share in His work*. Read that previous sentence as many times as necessary to let that concept sink in. God is not asking us to do His work. God is not asking us to only watch Him work. God is asking us to *work with Him*.

Nehemiah grasped this truth, and put it into practice. He did not shirk his responsibility, but put forth his best effort, in preparation, execution, and managing difficulties. He also knew that the task and ultimate success belonged to God. Nehemiah was a steward, working with God to seek success. So Nehemiah bathed all his efforts in prayer to ensure that he was maintaining his proper role in his partnership with God.

## Building a Blended Response

We all have a bias toward either action or inaction. There is no "right" bias, as either extreme can do harm. The important thing is to know yourself and understand which particular side you tend towards, especially in times of stress. Then seek God's help in moving you toward a better blend of prayer and action.

I have an analytical nature, which can lead to errors in either direction. First, my bias is toward analysis over action, which makes me seek God and even wait on God. So, I can fall into "analysis paralysis," in which I study, study, study, like the "ready, aim. Aim," quote at the beginning of the chapter. I wait for God without taking any direct action (or responsibility) for the work at hand. On the other hand, I can place too much trust in my analytical skills, leading me, once I have completed my analysis, to strike off on my own, as if I am responsible for the success of my endeavor, without leaning on God or preceding all my post-analysis actions with prayer.

We must view our life in Christ as ongoing invitations in two directions. First, God graciously invites us to be involved in His work. This often involves setting a specific responsibility before us as part of His kingdom work. This amazing invitation moves us from the position of spectator to being actively involved in God's business. Second, we must continually invite God to guide us through our work for Him. This invitation to God is extended by means of constant prayer. We must continually seek God's direction and aid as we carry out our responsibility.

> God has chosen to use the Church as His primary instrument for accomplishing His will during this age.

We must never forget that God's invitation to us was a *partnership*, not a handoff. Our efforts must always be preceded by and bathed in prayer. The proper blend of waiting on God and our own decision-making comes by practice and maturity. Do not be troubled if early efforts cause a slide to either side. God is a patient teacher, ready to gently correct us and guide us back to the proper path.

The best summary is to view our relationship with God as a submitted partnership. God is sovereign over all things, including our daily lives. But He desires our active involvement and best effort in working with Him. Nehemiah understood that relationship and worked with God while submitting the results to direction by God.

## Practical Lordship in Action

The average Christian understands that Jesus Christ is to be Lord, but how does that work in an ongoing relationship between us and the Lord of the Universe? These principles form a good foundation from which we can operate.

1) Jesus Christ sits at the right hand of God. We must first acknowledge God's holiness and transcendence. He exists on an entirely different plane from us, on a completely different level.
2) We are joint heirs with Christ, called to share in His suffering so that we might also share in His blessings. Jesus as God incarnate has chosen to share portions of His ministry with us.
3) We are to die to self each day, and live for Christ. Our goals should be aligned with God's goals. We should not charge off and "do things for God." We need to be walking *with* God.

4) God has called each of us to specific ministry. This calling is not necessarily vocational. This may be at our work places, with our families, or related to hobbies or community activities. But God has called us all to do things in His kingdom.

> We should not charge off and 'do things for God.' We need to be walking *with* God.

5) The most effective way to work for God and with God is through blending this activity with prayer. This keeps us tethered to God's purposes, so that our efforts do not morph into our own agenda.

It is easiest to seek God's direction when trying to follow Him in the first place. If we enter into an activity in a state of rebellion, we are less likely to seek God's blessing and guidance. We must always check our motivation to guarantee that our goal is to do things *with* God rather than *for* God.

# Prayer Building Block #9:
## Seek a balanced partnership with God.

## Are you trying to walk with God?

Or do you run ahead and try to do everything on your own strength, not wanting to "bother" God? On the other hand, do you wait for God to act so that you do not have to take any action? When in trouble, do you try to fight your way out on your own, or do you wait for God to rescue you?

God wants neither lone rangers nor spectators. He wants partners, submitted to Him while actively working with Him. The best way to partner with God is to seek God in prayer as part of saturating your actions in prayer. A balanced and healthy partnership with God will blend both action and prayer, recognizing that there will be situations where one or the other will take precedence.

Nehemiah recognized this dynamic and modeled it throughout his life. There were times when he waited on God in prayer, as demonstrated in Nehemiah chapter one. But when it was time to take action, he had a plan ready to implement. He also sought God prior to taking action, confident that, as he was fulfilling his calling from God, he could proceed under God's blessing as he continually sought God in prayer.

Pray and act. Keep the two together.

# Chapter 10

# Praying under Opposition

"I will execute great vengeance on them with wrathful rebukes.
Then they will know that I am the LORD,
when I lay my vengeance upon them."
*– God, Ezekiel 25:17*[1]

Wouldn't it be fun to call down curses on your enemies? When people taunt and ridicule you, to invoke the power of God on your behalf? When others try to block you from success or even intend you harm, wouldn't it be satisfying to unleash God as the ultimate Big Brother to do to them as they plotted to do to you, in a reverse Golden Rule? You could sit back and laugh as they received their comeuppance.

Then the naysayers spoil it all by quoting scripture: "Vengeance is mine; I will repay" (Rom. 12:19), reminding us that only God has the authority to judge and punish others. But it was a fun dream while it lasted.

Or was it?

We are caught between the truth behind Christ telling us, "if you ask me anything in my name, I will do it" (John 14:13) and the knowing we cannot seek punishment of others. So how do we handle dealing with our enemies—and our very human response—while not being disobedient to God and continuing to build relationship with Him through prayer? Nehemiah faced this very same problem, and his response can instruct our prayer lives.

# Ridicule and Opposition

Work on rebuilding the Jerusalem wall proceeded quickly, after the initial inspection and organization of the effort. But just as today, some people do not like others to succeed, especially when the "others" represented someone they bullied for years. It would be harder to pick on the Israelites if they could defend themselves behind a completed city wall.

So, in Nehemiah chapter four, they began a pattern of ridicule and mockery. They belittled the effort, which was not hard, since the Israelites were reusing old burned stones to rebuild the wall, rather than a fresh supply. They mocked the anticipated final result, stating the wall would not hold up even under small animals scurrying about, much less deter an invading army. These insults were meant to discourage the workers and cause them to give up the effort.

We experience this today. We muster the will to make a positive change, and the mockery begins. We're told we won't see any lasting difference from our efforts, and that any attempt at permanent improvement will be futility for us, while providing entertainment through our folly for others.

How do we handle the discouragement while struggling to make a change in our lives? Every setback fulfills the prophecy of our tormentors. We wish they would just go away, but they insist on hanging around, ready to pounce on every problem, or just being an anchor to drag down our efforts at progress. Maybe God can make them go away. Permanently.

# Right Back at Them

Nehemiah's response was to pray an imprecatory prayer, which calls upon God to bring down curses upon one's enemies. These prayers were common in Old Testament times for all peoples, not just the Israelites, with a tone similar to this: "Hear, O our God, for we are despised. Turn back their taunt on their own heads and give them up to be plundered in a land where they are captives. Do not cover their guilt, and let not their sin be blotted out from your sight, for they have provoked you to anger in the presence of the builders" (Neh. 4:4–5).

First, Nehemiah reminded God of the Israelites' lowly status in the eyes of, well, everyone else. Second, he asked for the insults of their mockers to be turned back on them, for *them* to receive what they dished out to the Israelites rebuilding the wall. Then he took it further. Nehemiah requested his mockers receive the same judgment given to Israel for disobeying God, namely, requesting that they be taken captive and led into exile. Finally, he asked for the mockers to receive God's eternal judgment, seeking they be declared guilty for their sins, stating that their actions had angered God Himself. These curses comprised some pretty stern stuff. Nehemiah, a godly man of prayer, asked God to do these things on the Israelites' behalf.

> Nehemiah saw the mockers as not just attacking the people but attacking God Himself.

We all can feel this way. We want bad things to happen to our enemies. We wish for people to receive the bad actions they intend for us. And we wish God would somehow consider them less righteous than us and punish them accordingly, because how dare they pick on and bully us!

But significantly, observe what Nehemiah did after he prays. After praying for punishment upon his mockers, Nehemiah went forth and … did **nothing**. He made no attempt to follow up on his prayer. He did not report them to the authorities. He did not plot to get back at them or seek vengeance.

## Three Types of Opposition

Dealing with opposition from people will always be one of the byproducts of sin. We delude ourselves if we pretend situations will not exist in which we encounter problems, as did Nehemiah. How this sin plays out in people can be divided into three categories.

First are the sinfully ignorant, those who unwittingly do bad things to others. They may be boorish, crass, or outright mean, but they lack self-awareness concerning the results of their actions on others. Like a bull in a china shop, they unintentionally inflict damage on their surroundings without comprehending their impact. Residual pain on others is not a specific goal. Damage to us occurs because we happen to be in their way, not because we are a target of their ill will.

Second are the mockers, who treat all of life as a joke, and we are merely their latest punch line. Ever cynical, they belittle others' efforts, laugh at any progress, and celebrate others' failures. Never seeking change or improvement themselves, they drift through life, ready to derail anyone else's progress. While they seek to deliberately harm others, their entire arsenal consists of verbal weapons. We may be the victims of deliberate verbal assaults, but that is the normal limit of their abuse.

Finally, there are the truly malevolent. Whether evil at the core or just acting on animosity directed toward a specific person or group, they seek to intentionally harm the target of their wrath. They will plot to destroy their target's efforts, use any connections to undermine progress, and work to undo what others have done. Their goal is the destruction of another's efforts, and sometimes the complete ruin of that person. With them it is personal, and they do intend to do harm.

The mockers Nehemiah faced in Nehemiah chapters four and six were in the latter two categories. They were intentionally trying to thwart the wall-building efforts. When their threats and mockery proved unsuccessful, they resorted to plots and even attempted character assassination. They had two goals: to stop the wall from being rebuilt and to render Nehemiah ineffective for any future leadership among the people of Israel.

## An Overreaction?

When the mockers tried to stop the wall building, Nehemiah understood they were trying to halt more than just a team-building exercise. The Israelites felt abandoned by God, even as they had returned to the Promised Land. Their capital city stood vulnerable to attack, and their rebuilt Temple remained equally defenseless. Nehemiah had raised their hopes that the wall could be rebuilt and God honored by the result.

So, Nehemiah's response in bringing down curses upon his mockers must be seen in light of the bigger issue. This project was more than just a wall; this effort represented a future where God would, indeed, bless Israel once again and reestablish relationship with His chosen people. With the backing of the Persian king, the timing was perfect to complete what had been so long neglected. Nehemiah saw the mockers as not just attacking the people but attacking *God Himself.*

Nehemiah became demonstrably angry at the attempt to block what he understood to be God's plan. We do not talk like this publicly in our hyper-sensitive culture, but at one time people felt free to express their feelings of frustration and anger. Nehemiah was a man of prayer. But this particular prayer had sharp teeth and claws.

## Trusting God

To understand how Nehemiah could be a godly man of prayer and still pray in this manner, we must understand the process Nehemiah followed. He may have rehearsed his response, or it became the result of many years of turning to God prior to taking action. We must understand this process as we seek to rebuild our relationship with God in prayer.

First, Nehemiah expressed his feelings to God. He did not hold back. He did not outwardly pretend "everything is fine" while inwardly seething. He did not lie to God and declare the mocking and insults irrelevant while plotting his revenge. Nehemiah laid his feelings bare before the Lord, telling God how he felt, not what he thought God wanted to hear.

**Nehemiah left his anger with God.**

Second, Nehemiah sought help from God. From the beginning, Nehemiah depended on God's favor and provision, even if God was using humans as His surrogates. So in this time of crisis, he yet again placed his need before God. Nehemiah faithfully trusted that the God who launched this venture would see the Israelites through any difficulties arising from taking the initial steps of faith. In short, Nehemiah trusted God.

Third, Nehemiah left his anger with God. Scripture does not record any revenge or pre-emptive strike by Nehemiah against his attackers. Nehemiah continued at his task, making adjustments based upon subsequent opposition. He did not let the mocking and threats deter him from his goal of rebuilding the wall. So, after expressing his anger to God, Nehemiah did nothing to act upon his initial angry feelings.

Finally, Nehemiah left future judgment and punishment of the mockers up to God. As much as he may have been tempted to advise God on matters of judgment, Nehemiah knew God alone has the authority to judge men. His trust of God allowed him to not intrude where he did not belong. His prayerfulness had brought him to knowing God's character and trusting in God's justice and righteousness. His honest—if harsh—prayer had again brought him into close relationship with God, intimately sharing his deepest feelings, however raw.

While not having experienced the level of mockery and attack Nehemiah underwent, I can sympathize with his feelings. Years ago, co-workers attempted to sabotage my career, trying to keep me from promotions or even remove me from a project. I had people talk sweetly to my face while gossiping behind my back to others. Worst of all (to me), I experienced others opposing and even seeking ill for my wife and children. Those attacks cut the deepest, and I wanted to pray the same prayer as Nehemiah did, perhaps adding some slow torture for special effect.

But I knew bitterness and rage were wrong, and I sought to follow Nehemiah's pattern of venting and then leaving it with God. Even if it took hundreds of prayers, I knew I would draw closer to God through communicating my anger honestly and trusting God rather than giving in to my anger and acting out. God is Lord over all, including opposition I might face as I seek to follow God.

# Prayer Building Block #10:
## Take your anger to God and leave it with Him.

## How do you respond when attacked, either verbally, or someone directly plotting against you?

Do you seek retribution, or just simmer inside and let bitterness take root? Do you express your anger to God, or avoid God due to embarrassment over your harsh or even sinful feelings? (News flash: God already knows how you feel, so avoiding Him to hide your feelings will not work.)

Our culture teaches a twisted version of the Golden Rule, encouraging us to "do unto others *before* they do unto us." We remain defensive, ready to lash out at the slightest provocation. We separate ourselves from others to remain safe, even as we separate ourselves from God, not believing He is willing or able to minister to us when we are attacked.

Perhaps we even resent God for past attacks, wondering how a benevolent God could allow bad things to happen to good people. Explaining the why is beyond the scope of this discussion. We can only acknowledge the seemingly incompatible propositions: 1) there is a sovereign good God, and 2) there is sin manifested through sinful people in the world.

Nehemiah knew and accepted both of these truths. He also knew any intimate relationship needed to be strong enough to handle all honest feelings and thoughts, however brutal. So he took his brutally honest feelings to God in prayer. Then, because he also understood the sovereignty of God, he left his feelings with God and continued in the task to which God had called him.

## It comes down to honesty and trust.

Are you honest enough to take your worst feelings and thoughts to God? And do you trust God enough to accept how He will resolve your situation with your opposition? In prior chapters of this book, we learned how Nehemiah blended actions with his prayers. But now we must focus on leaving our negative feelings with God.

Honesty and trust. In order to rebuild your relationship with God, to take it to a deeper level, you need to be ready to take everything, even your emotional garbage, to God. But then, we must leave it with God instead of using it to fuel revenge or bitterness. Your situation might require taking it to God hundreds of times (or even more). God will be ready to receive it every single time you bring it to Him. Nehemiah built his trust in and relationship with God through years of continual prayer. Therefore, when attacked, he could respond in a human but godly manner. Nehemiah did not deny or repress his feelings. He took them and surrendered them to God.

Instead of lashing back against your attackers, through prayer give your anger—and your opponents—over to God.

# Chapter 11

# Praying under Personal Attack

"It's hard to be religious when certain people are
never incinerated by bolts of lightning."
– *Calvin, Calvin and Hobbes*[1]

There was once a young man, sitting in prison, likely wondering why people kept attacking him. It began with his brothers. They were jealous of him and his plans for success. Of course, it did not help when he announced that one day that they, his older brothers, would bow down to him. They sold him into slavery and lied to their father about his death.

He was able to make slavery tolerable by working hard and gaining the trust of the head of the house, who placed everything under his care. His hard work blessed the household, and life, while not free, was fairly comfortable. But his master's wife had designs on him, seeking to engage in illicit relations with him while his master was away. After repeatedly rebuffing her advances, he found that his only option was to flee from her presence, leaving his cloak in her hands. Enraged by the rejection, the wife lied about being attacked by the young man. The master angrily threw the young man into prison to spend the remainder of his days, however brief. How had his life come to this state? Why did everyone seem to be personally against him?

The young man is Joseph from the Genesis account. And yes, the attacks were personal. His brothers resented Joseph telling them that he would one day rule over them. Older brothers did not serve younger brothers in that culture! Then the enraged wife of his master, upset that Joseph had rejected her advances, lied about who was seeking the infidelity, causing Joseph to be unjustly thrown into prison. While guilty of no sin, but perhaps immature in how he interacted with his brothers, Joseph had become the target of personal attacks. Now he was in prison, with no apparent way out. How does he respond to his attackers? How does he turn to God for mercy and justice when his experience has seemingly been the opposite?

Nehemiah faced a similar situation while rebuilding the Jerusalem wall. After their enemies' efforts to halt the wall-building had been thwarted through prayer and action, Nehemiah's opponents tried a different approach. This time they went after Nehemiah personally.

# The Leader is a Target

The simple position of being a leader places a target on the leader's back. In *The Patriot*, General Cornwallis asked the Mel Gibson character to instruct his men to stop shooting at British officers. But Gibson's Benjamin Martin was following a common military practice. The best way to disrupt an army was to eliminate those in charge. The men might be able to continue in small groups led at the local level, but there would be no coordinated effort and they could easily be overwhelmed by a well-led force.

Both Nehemiah and his opponents knew the precarious nature of the wall-building effort. After all, no one had stepped up to lead such an activity before Nehemiah arrived on the scene. Earlier threats had caused the people to waver until Nehemiah rallied them to refocus on their efforts as he took measures to guarantee their safety. Without Nehemiah's drive, the effort to rebuild the Jerusalem wall could quickly collapse and fail.

It made sense for the opposition to go after Nehemiah, because the success of the venture rested on him. Of course, Nehemiah knew that their success rested entirely on God, but even if his opponents believed in God, they saw Nehemiah as the only Israelite who could effectively summon the power and perseverance of God. If they wanted to stop the wall-building, they had to stop Nehemiah.

Nehemiah chapter six records three specific personal attacks launched in turn upon Nehemiah, along with his response to each attack. As we read in the previous chapter here, although personally frustrated and angered by the attacks, Nehemiah did not plot revenge or hold a grudge, but gave over his opponents and their actions to God for judgment.

## Personal Attack #1: Physical Harm

The first attempt at attack occurred when Nehemiah's opponents sent a message to him saying, "Come and let us meet together at Hakkephirim in the plain of Ono" (Neh. 6:2). This area was about seven miles southeast of Joppa, in the westernmost area settled by the returning Israelites.[2] In other words, many miles from Jerusalem. Their intent could not be more clear if they had written an engraved invitation, and Nehemiah saw through this: "But they intended to do me harm" (Neh. 6:2).

Why would his opponents attempt such a clumsy and transparent ruse? Scripture does not say. But it does record Nehemiah's polite but firm rebuff: "And I sent messengers to them saying, 'I am doing a great work and I cannot come down. Why should the work stop while I leave it and come down to you?'" (Neh. 6:3). Nehemiah did not call them on the physical threat he knew was behind the invitation. But he refused to consider their request.

> Nehemiah did not plot revenge or hold a grudge, but gave over his opponents and their actions to God for judgment.

Nehemiah's enemies tried this ploy four times, and Nehemiah rejected their request four times. Why did they persist in this type of attack? Because it is the simplest. It takes plenty of planning and foresight and subtlety to coordinate other attacks on reputation or character. Only brute force is needed for a physical attack. It is the most straightforward method of eliminating an opponent. But it only works if you can get your opponent into a vulnerable position. Nehemiah refused to take the bait and expose himself to danger. This method of attack was clearly not going to work.

## Personal Attack #2: Rumors

The vicious effectiveness of rumors is you can ruin someone's cause without even touching them. You do not even have to interact with them, but simply carry the rumors to others who will listen. These rumors do not even need to be remotely connected to the truth. In fact, wild rumors can be more effective than a mere stretching of the truth.

Their effectiveness lies in the time and energy that combating the rumors drains from the actual effort. Every minute spent putting out fires started by rumors is time not spent advancing the stated goals. If too much attention needs to be diverted to managing rumors, the entire project might come to a halt.

This was the ploy used by Sanballat and the other opponents when they sent word to Nehemiah a fifth time. The first four messages were thinly disguised attempts to get Nehemiah away from Jerusalem to where he could be harmed. Seeing they could not dislodge him from his focus on building the wall, they sent notice of their next attempt to distract Nehemiah:

> "It is reported among the nations, and Geshem also says it, that you and the Jews intend to rebel; that is why you are building the wall. And according to these reports you wish to become their king. And you have also set up prophets to proclaim concerning you in Jerusalem, 'There is a king in Judah.' And now the king will hear of these reports. So now come and let us take counsel together" (Neh. 6:6–7).

That was a sly attack based on past history. When Zerubbabbel was rebuilding the Temple after the Exile, reports were sent back to the king in Persia that he intended to declare himself king and rebel. So he was removed and the Temple rebuilding effort delayed for twenty years. Israel had a history of being restive and chafing under foreign control. An insecure king might believe the rumors, however unfounded, and put a stop to the efforts.

Nehemiah could easily refute this rumor, and said: "No such things as you say have been done, for you are inventing them out of your own mind" (Neh. 6:8). Nehemiah knew the rumors were so outrageous that he could easily counter them. He spent years in personal contact with the king, and had the king's trust. This would not be undermined by wild accusations. The attempt to get Nehemiah to stop his work by forcing him to address rumors also failed.

However, facing attacks, even if they can be repelled successfully, is very draining. It saps the energy and starts to sap the soul. A weariness sets in, and it becomes more difficult to continue functioning, to both successfully complete the project and fend off attacks. It is very difficult, if not impossible, to continue both efforts using human strength. So Nehemiah turned again to God, seeking the strength he needed to deal with the personal attacks: "But now, O God, strengthen my hands" (Neh. 6:9).

Some have questioned whether this is a prayer, since the original Hebrew does not specifically mention God. Some scholars see it as a personal resolve of Nehemiah to strengthen his hands. But the imperative form of the verb translated "strengthen" indicates that Nehemiah is speaking to someone other than himself.[3] And responding in prayer matches the

> Nehemiah turned again to God, seeking the strength he needed to deal with the personal attacks.

pattern already established by Nehemiah to react to any and all obstacles with prayer first. We can comfortably conclude that Nehemiah is seeking God's strength through prayer, just as he continually seeks God's aid in all situations in his memoirs.

## Personal Attack #3: Credibility

When you cannot attack someone personally and you cannot attack their work, then you attack their credibility and reputation. That was the motive behind the third attack on Nehemiah by his enemies. Many people make poor decisions under pressure, so they tried to pressure Nehemiah into a reputation-destroying decision: "Let us meet together in the house of God, within the temple. Let us close the doors of the temple, for they are coming to kill you. They are coming to kill you by night" (Neh. 6:10).

Now the threat of physical harm, not stated in the first attack, was used directly to goad Nehemiah into a bad action. What was bad about going into the Temple? Because Nehemiah was not qualified to enter the Temple, as he stated when he replied: "Should such a man as I run away? And what man such as I could go into the temple and live? I will not go in" (Neh. 6:11).

Temple worship had been specifically set up by God so that only the Levites, and specifically descendants of Aaron, could enter the Temple. Going against this meant severe punishment. When Israel under David was returning the Ark to the Tabernacle, they used a cart instead of Levites carrying it on poles so as not to touch it. So when it naturally began to slip off the cart and someone instinctively reached out to catch it, he was struck dead. This may seem harsh, but Israel had violated God's specific instructions for handling the Ark.

In fact, a primary reason for the Exile was sinfulness involving how Israel regarded items God considered to be holy, including the Temple. This sinfulness was recognized during the Exile, and some of the later legalism can be traced to building a "law around the Law" so as not to go against God's commandments.

So, it was clear about who got to enter the Temple, and Nehemiah knew he was not qualified. Scripture does not record the reason for his disqualification. One common theory is that Nehemiah was a eunuch, since many servants of ancients kings were so altered, and anyone mutilated was not able to minister within the Temple. This is not conclusive and is conjecture. Another common theory is that Nehemiah was not a descendent of Aaron, but this is not known either, as his recorded lineage goes back no further than his father Hacaliah. Even if Nehemiah was of the proper lineage, he would not have been ceremonially prepared to enter the Temple per proper worship instructions.

Plus, even if he were qualified, fleeing to the Temple for safety would undermine all Nehemiah's prior encouraging talk to the Israelites to remain at their task despite the danger. He knew the irreparable damage this would do to his reputation: "For this purpose he was hired, that I should be afraid and act in this way and sin, and so they could give me a bad name in order to taunt me" (Neh. 6:13). Once Nehemiah's name was ruined, he could no longer be a credible leader, and the wall-building effort would fail.

Nehemiah's final response to these attacks is similar to an earlier imprecatory prayer: "Remember Tobiah and Sanballat, O my God, according to these things that they did, and also the prophetess Noadiah and the rest of the prophets who wanted to make me afraid" (Neh. 6:14). Nehemiah did not seek revenge. He simply handed them over to God.

## Handling Personal Attacks

Seeing Nehemiah in action deflecting these attacks provides several lessons for us in responding to similar attacks today. First, do not panic. Many bad decisions can be made if we do not first stop and gather ourselves. For

Nehemiah, this always included stopping to pray before taking any action or making any decision.

Second, do not take personal attacks personally. Sometimes you may represent something opposed by someone else, rather than their personal enmity against you. Nehemiah represented the wall-building effort, to which others were opposed. They did not regard Nehemiah personally, just as the agent leading an effort they wanted to stop. You might feel a personal attack from someone who is opposed to God, and you are the nearest representative they can attack.

Third, always seek God's help. It might be wisdom in dealing with these attacks, or simply strength to carry on. Nehemiah knew that success depended upon God and continually went to Him for help.

> **Nehemiah did not seek revenge. He simply handed them over to God.**

Fourth, do not be afraid. People can threaten us and even harm us, but God's purposes will prevail. We have no knowledge of the length of our days, but we can honor and serve God throughout their duration. Nehemiah recognized this truth and did not respond in fear of others but by faith in God.

Finally, do not let personal attacks distract you from your original task, which was the reason for the attack in the first place. Even if you successfully blunt attacks and emerge with your body or reputation intact, but did not complete what you set out to do, your opponents won. For their goal was not to attack you but to stop you from what you were doing. Nehemiah recognized this and did not let up on his wall-building efforts. We see the results after the final attack was thwarted: "So the wall was finished on the twenty-fifth day of the month Elul, in fifty-two days" (Neh. 6:15).

# Prayer Building Block #11:
## When under attack, seek God for strength.

## If you are ever under attack you must resist the urge to get down to your opponent's level and fight back.

It will end up like wrestling with a pig: even if you win, you still look foolish and get dirty. I wish I had always personally followed this advice, but I had times when my human anger overwhelmed my spirit (and common sense), and I lashed back.

Rather, follow Nehemiah's example and seek God for strength. While he personally wished ill on his opponents, he left all judgment up to God, and left the matter of dealing with them to God.

Why? Because God had called him to a task, and any effort—even pursuing what could be considered justice—would deter him from accomplishing what God had called him to. Nehemiah wanted to be faithful to God more than he wanted vengeance. That is where our hearts must lie also.

Instead of revenge, Nehemiah sought strength from God, strength to endure the attacks and still complete his calling. This did not mean he did nothing about the attacks. But he dismissed them quickly to return to his primary focus.

## What is God calling you to do?

Are you steady at the task, or do you keep getting distracted? Do you spend more time responding to your opponents than making progress on your goals? Are you slowly getting burned out because of working in your own strength?

Stop getting sidetracked. Focus on God and what you are called to do. Seek to walk with God in all your days, handing your opposition over to Him to deal with and ultimately judge.

Most of all, continually and prayerfully seek God's strength.

# Chapter 12

# Praying Scripture

*"We are, in truth, more than half what we are by imitation.*
*The great point is, to choose good models and to study them with care."*
*– Lord Chesterfield*[1]

Each week, many churches recite The Lord's Prayer during their
worship services. It may be a ritual, or it may be heartfelt, but it occurs with
great frequency. It is also recited before football games and other public
events. It is likely the most recognizable prayer in all of Christendom.

Why not? The prayer came from Jesus. In Luke, it was a response to a
request from the disciples to "teach us to pray" (Luke 11:1). In Matthew,
when Jesus was teaching on prayer, He instructed to pray not like the
hypocrites or pagans. He then said, "Pray then like this:" (Matt. 6:9). Both
passages then give what is commonly known as The Lord's Prayer. Jesus was
clearly teaching a proper way to pray.

Are we to use the exact words in the prayer recorded in Scripture, or
follow the ideas expressed in the prayer while using our own words? The
answer is yes to both. Since all of Scripture is inspired by God, we can easily
align our thoughts and requests with God's will by repeating the actual words.
But we can also use the biblical concepts reflected in the text as a basis for
personalizing our prayers to God.

Nehemiah understood how the most effective means of aligning our
prayers with God's will was to use God's own words and concepts. So his
prayers, particularly the prayer recorded in Nehemiah 1:5–11, borrowed
heavily from Scripture. He knew that, to speak to God and not be influenced

by a personal agenda, prayer needed to be influenced by God. This is done most easily through the use of Scripture when praying.

## Praying the Exact Words

Since the prayer in Nehemiah 1:5–11 is the most extensive prayer of Nehemiah recorded, it is the one we will use to demonstrate how Nehemiah was influenced by Scripture when he prayed. The following table shows actual phrases in this prayer that were taken from other portions of Scripture, recognizing that, due to translations, some texts will be more word-for-word than others.

| Verse in Nehemiah | Phrase | Verse(s) found elsewhere |
|---|---|---|
| 1:5 | "the great and awesome God" | Deut. 7:21; Deut. 10:17 |
| 1:5 | "who keeps covenant and steadfast love with those who love him and keep his commandments" | Deut. 5:10; Deut. 7:9; 1 Kings 8:23 |
| 1:6 | "let your ear be attentive and your eyes open, to hear the prayer…" | 1 Kings 8:29; 1 Kings 8:52; 2 Chron. 6:40; 2 Chron. 7:15; Psalm 130:2 |
| 1:7 | "the commandments, the statutes, and the rules" | Deut. 5:31; Deut. 6:1; Deut. 7:11; Deut. 8:11 |
| 1:7 | "your servant Moses" | Deut. 34:5 |
| 1:9 | "to the place that I have chosen, to make my name dwell there" | Deut. 12:5; Deut. 12:11; Deut. 14:23; Deut. 16:6; Deut. 16:11; Deut. 26:2; 1 Kings 8:29; 1 Kings 8:44; 1 Chron. 22:7–10; 2 Chron. 6:5–9 |

| 1:11 | "who delight to fear your name" | Deut. 28:58 |

Chart 1: Word-for-word phrases in Nehemiah 1:5–11 found in other Old Testament texts.

Nehemiah had most of the Old Testament available to him, certainly the Pentateuch, the historical books, the Psalms, and most of the Prophets were recorded at this stage in history. He understood Israel's history, including both God's provision and judgment, and could see how Israel deserved judgment while he was seeking God's mercy.

> Nehemiah wanted to describe God's promises accurately, with no errors due to misinterpretation.

But why use the exact phrases? Wouldn't the basic idea be good enough? Most of the time, it would. But there are situations where the precise words matter. For example, in traditional wedding vows, the bride pledged to "love, honor, and obey" her husband. Most vows have been revised for the bride to "love, honor and *cherish*" her husband. One word means a big difference in relative roles and family hierarchy. Or take a promise to meet for lunch "someday," which is so open-ended it frequently means the opposite, compared to a commitment to schedule lunch "this week."

Note that the words quoted directly by Nehemiah center around God's Person and God's Promises. In the first case, Nehemiah wanted to be sure he described God the way God describes himself. He wants an accurate portrayal of God's character and attributes. In the second case, Nehemiah wanted to ensure that he described God's promises accurately, with no errors due to misinterpretation. He did not want to miss anything, and he did not want to misspeak concerning what God promised to do for His people.

## Praying the Concept

While praying the exact phrases from Scripture keep us within God's will and from diverting into our own agenda, we do not need to be limited to the actual words. If we regularly read the Bible, we can be familiar with the concepts and thoughts without repeating word-for-word. The below table shows where Nehemiah's prayer in Nehemiah 1:5–11 has followed the ideas from other passages of Scripture.

| Verse in Nehemiah | Phrase | Verse(s) found elsewhere |
|---|---|---|
| 1:6–7 | Theme that the Exile was due to Israel's disobedience | Psalm 74; Psalm 79 |
| 1:8b | Theme of being scattered among the nations | Deut. 28:64; Jer. 9:16; Ezek. 11:16; Ezek. 12:15; Ezek. 20:23; Ezek. 22:15; Ezek. 36:19 |
| 1:8b–9 | These verses are seen as a summary of the Deuteronomy passage | Deut. 30:1–4 |
| 1:9 | Theme that God will gather Israel in after a season of judgment | Isa. 11:12; Jer. 23:3; Jer. 29:14; Ezek. 11:17; Ezek. 20:34; Ezek. 20:41; Ezek. 34:13; Ezek. 36:24 |
| 1:9 | Theme that God chose Jerusalem as a place to dwell | Psalm 132 |
| 1:10 | Theme of redemption by the strong hand of God— variations on "a mighty hand and outstretched arm" | Deut. 3:24; Deut. 4:34; Deut. 5:15; Deut. 7:8; Deut. 9:26; Deut. 9:29; 1 Kings 8:42; 1 Chron. 17:21; 2 Chron. 6:32; Psalm |

| | | 136:12; Jer. 27:5; Jer. 32:17; Ezek. 20:33 |
|---|---|---|
| 1:11 | Request that God grant success | Psalm 118:25 |

Chart 2: Concepts and themes in Nehemiah 1:5–11 found in other Old Testament texts.

These passages—beginning in Deuteronomy and continuing through history books, Psalms, and the Prophets—show these unifying themes persist throughout the Old Testament. Since Nehemiah was well-versed in the Scripture of his day, he naturally turned to the prevailing themes as a foundation for his prayers.

This option may be better than memorizing Scripture for future use in prayer. I personally have trouble with word-for-word memorization, but during prayer can recall a phrase from a passage, tying it to the full concept expressed. Sometimes focusing on the exact words may cause us to stumble, thinking that we must have them right, rather than the thing we are attempting to do, speaking with God. Knowing the concept means that we are staying true to God's will as expressed by Scripture in those times when we haven't fully memorized a selected passage.

# Praying a Scriptural Style

One fear people have about praying, especially praying in public, is that they do not sound eloquent. Some people feel they must break into King James' (Elizabethan) English with the corresponding *thees* and *thous*. Others feel they must seek to attain to some lofty and spiritual form of English. Feeling ill-prepared to assume either form of "proper" prayer, they become fearful and hesitant.

While certain biblical prayers seem well-thought-out and eloquent, such as Nehemiah's prayer in Nehemiah chapter one and Solomon's prayer of dedication for the Temple, we should not seek to replicate their language or formality. Nehemiah's prayer is considered a summary of his season of prayer. Solomon's prayer was part of a formal national service of dedication, and thus rightly formal. Instead, we should observe the content of these prayers over their word usage and seek to adopt their general format. In chapters three through seven, we already defined the form of Nehemiah's prayer. In this section, I hope to show that the form and style of Nehemiah's prayer was not unique and mirrored other biblical prayers, along with lessons we can learn by following a biblical prayer style.

First, we can begin our prayers with praise. Nehemiah opened his prayer, as did Solomon, by praising God. God's attributes, including mercy and provision, are emphasized. They both, along with Daniel, requested God's attention, an act of humility showing that they were seeking God. Part of this praise is describing what God has already done on behalf of His people.

Second, we can make confession an important foundation of our prayers. When Nehemiah focused on both personal and national confession of sins, he showed the same emphasis given in Daniel chapter nine. When Daniel prayed to God to find out what was planned next for Israel, since the 70-year Exile was nearing its completion, he opened with a similar praise and then entered into an extended time of confession, beginning at verse five and continuing through verse fifteen. It is the largest part of his prayer. While confession is not the bulk of Nehemiah's prayer, it takes up more space than his actual request. Both Daniel and Nehemiah knew that they had to deal with their sin before God would deal with their requests.

Third, we can remember God's promises. Both Nehemiah and Solomon repeat promises God had made to Israel, both for judgment and redemption. The confession and recognition of judgment naturally led into a request for mercy and redemption. God desires to be in fellowship with us, so reminding Him of His promises will help us to remember and trust God's promises in our lives.

Fourth, we can let God move us and change us. Many psalms are known as lament psalms, and begin with a thought of "How long, O Lord?" questioning how long they were to remain in their condition of suffering. Nehemiah can be seen to imply the same thought as he pleaded for God's mercies. But as the prayers progress, the writers are moved from a mood of sorrow to thankfulness for God's presence and a patient waiting on God. We can adopt the same spirit of humility, allowing God to work in us through our prayers and move us to where He wants us to be.

Finally, we can let God be God in our prayers. Too often we use our prayers to tell God what to do in a specific situation. Notice that none of the biblical prayers dictate to God. Rather, they present their request, seek God's mercy, but do not attempt to give God advice as to the best solution. Our prayers would be better served if we waited on God instead of giving orders to Him.

## Praying Scripture within Context

One big caution of using Scripture in prayers is the warning to keep Scripture within context. Many well-intentioned Christians end up distorting God's Word and will by removing a passage or phrase out of context and applying new meaning to the passage. This error can occur in all facets of Bible interpretation, and prayer is no exception.

For example, John 14:13 begins "Whatever you ask in my name, this I will do." We grab on to that almost as a talisman, that we get anything we ask for anything in Jesus' name. So, we append the phrase "in Jesus' name" to our prayers, hoping that the magic words will cause God to grant our request. (Note: Not everyone is using this phrase as a mantra, and many Christians use it to ask for God's will and blessing on their requests.) But a look at the context shows the true meaning of "praying in Jesus' name":

"Truly, truly, I say to you, whoever believes in me will also do the works that I do; and greater works than these will he do, because I am going to the Father. Whatever you ask in my name, this I will do, that the Father may be glorified in the Son" (John 14:12-13).

The first step is obedience to God, as demonstrated by doing the works that Jesus did. At the conclusion, the purpose of Jesus answering the requests is to glorify God. The context of the larger passage is obedience to God and love for one another. At no point is it implied that praying in Jesus' name is the secret code to getting our prayers answered. Once Jesus returns to the Father, we are His visible representatives on earth. So, to "ask in [Jesus'] name" does not mean to append a phrase to your prayers, but to approach God, seeking help to fulfill your role as Christ's ambassador on earth.

Another passage misused by well-meaning parents is found in Proverbs 22:6: "Train up a child in the way he should go; even when he is old he will not depart from it." Many long-suffering Christians have used this verse as a promise that their children, no matter how wayward, will at some point turn their lives over to God if they had been raised in a Christian home. First of all, the Bible records far too many godly parents who sired evil children for this to be some sort of guarantee. Next, this verse is embedded in a section focusing on general good living and character, and not a specific spiritual decision to surrender to God. Finally, the phrase "way he should go" does not refer to a spiritual decision but a child's natural bent, meaning what they are naturally good at and enjoy. Once these factors are realized, the verse points not to a promise of salvation for our children, but wisdom in guiding them to what they enjoy and are skilled at, so that they might live happy and productive lives.[2] Obviously, their eternal destiny is found in Christ, but this verse is focusing on general well-being than eternal salvation, and it is a guide, not a promise.

> As you glean precepts from Scripture, understand them within the larger context.

This practice of keeping Scripture within context should be applied to our whole lives, not just our prayer lives. I have given two examples of verses at risk of being misused. When you memorize Scripture, be sure to understand the verse within its context to have the intended meaning as you carry it with you. As you glean precepts from Scripture, understand them within the larger context. Nehemiah drew upon themes running throughout the Bible, which is a good guide for us. Interpretations focused on one verse and not supported elsewhere are risky. The whole Bible is a unified account of God's love and redemption. As we pray, let us hold to God's word, not distorting or twisting it for our own benefit.

# Prayer Building Block #12:
## Know Scripture and use it in your prayers.

### How familiar are you with the Bible and its teachings?

It is hard to pray using Scripture if you do not *know* Scripture. Do you read the Bible regularly? Do you meditate on what you have read, allowing it to work into your person? Are you gaining in your knowledge of the Bible, both specific verses and prevailing themes and concepts?

Nehemiah demonstrated his knowledge of God's word through its heavy usage in his prayers, through both specific phrases and general concepts. The fact that he was a lay person and not a priest reinforces his piety, as he was not bound by his position to know Scripture, but chose to learn it as part of following God.

Nehemiah not only knew specific passages of the Bible but understood the larger account recorded there, how it revealed God's covenant history for Israel in both promise and judgment. He saw God at work, and rightly assumed that God was not done working based on both God's track record and promises for the future. He understood the sweep of history as God interacted with Israel.

### If you do not already do so, establish a pattern of regular Bible reading, both individual verses for meditation and longer passages to learn the progressive revelation of God's redemptive plan for all mankind.

Do not expect to quickly become an expert, but let God steadily work His Word and truth into you, developing a greater familiarity with the Bible as you build a greater intimacy with God.

As you rebuild your prayer life, bring God's word into your prayers. Start with praise because it is easy to recite, or even read, God's amazing character attributes. Expand the use of Scripture into all facets of your prayer life, seeking to align yourself with God by using His Word to guide you. As you center your thought life around the truth found in the Bible, you will find your prayers centering around God's will and plan for your life, jettisoning your personal agenda in favor of daily surrender to God.

Read God's word. Know God's word. Pray God's word.

## Chapter 13

# Seeking God's Remembrance

*"Remember me, O my God, for good."*
*– Nehemiah 13:31*

James Dobson is a Christian leader fighting for family and Christian values in modern society, but when he was younger, he was a skilled athlete. He won tennis tournaments in his college days, and a trophy bearing his name proudly sat in a display case at his college. A few years back, when the college was undergoing renovations, Dobson received a call. It seems they were disposing of the trophy but chose to contact him first to see if he wanted it before they threw it away. A trophy for what he considered a notable achievement was now being tossed in the trash![1]

Then there is the case of Fred "Bonehead" Merkle. Although he had a long Major League baseball career and was considered a good player, he is remembered through his nickname of a baserunning error committed while still a seldom-played teenager. Because his blunder was perceived to cost the Giants the pennant, the moniker was attached and overshadowed a very solid career. One mistake negated all the subsequent years of good baseball.[2]

We like to think our achievements will be remembered and appreciated by those following us in history. We also hope that the good things are not overshadowed by some spectacular blunder, so that any memory of us is not in infamy. But we ultimately have no control over how we are remembered.

Because Nehemiah knew history, he knew that deeds done during one generation were often forgotten by the next. Acts of obedience to God could be suppressed and ignored by future sinful generations. Each new age seemed intent on elevating itself by diminishing what had been done previously. So, Nehemiah did not place much trust in men to remember what he had achieved by rebuilding the Jerusalem wall and instituting religious reforms to prevent the people from returning to the sins that had caused their Exile.

Instead, Nehemiah looked to God for remembrance. The opinions of what other people thought about him did not matter so much as what God thought about him. So, at the end of his memoirs, Nehemiah seeks to be remembered by God for what he had done in his life. He trusted God to maintain an honest and just view of his life. In doing so, he built a legacy of prayer and God-centeredness that we can follow today.

## The Quest for Significance

Nehemiah first sought God's remembrance after helping ensure that the offerings were handled with integrity: "Remember me, O my God, concerning this, and do not wipe out my good deeds that I have done for the house of my God and for his service" (Neh. 13:14). After completing the rebuilding of the Jerusalem wall, Nehemiah carried out religious reforms, including insuring provision for those who ministered in the Temple. Nehemiah wanted to be sure that his efforts to do good on behalf of others were noticed by God. Nehemiah wanted to know that what he did was significant.

> **Nehemiah looked to God for remembrance.**

The quest for significance is common for people, and can be more difficult to attain in our throwaway age. Less and less of what we do is lasting. Anyone in the food service industry sees their efforts consumed within minutes. Even my background as a computer programmer produced little, if anything, of a lasting nature. We joke that everything we write is eventually rewritten by someone else who maligns our efforts while proclaiming their new product as superior.

So, we seek significance in things or events that cannot be discarded, but where can that be? In the things of God. Everything in this world will pass away, and only what is done for God will last. Nehemiah understood that achievements can be completed and good deeds done. God can remember them, even if they are undone by someone in the future.

Our accomplishments can be replaced, and our trophies discarded. Fortunately for us, God does not require mementos to remember the good done in His name. He will see and know all. Nehemiah knew that, but prayed to ensure that the motive and results of his efforts were understood and remembered.

# The Quest for Mercy

Nehemiah's second remembrance prayer is after recounting his efforts to honor the Sabbath: "Remember this also in my favor, O my God, and spare me according to the greatness of your steadfast love" (Neh. 13:22). Spare me? Nehemiah was seeking for God to spare him?

Look more closely at how Nehemiah hoped for God to spare him: "according to the greatness of your steadfast love." Nehemiah was appealing to God's mercy, for only through God's mercy could love be sustained and Nehemiah—or anyone else for that matter—be spared. The reason Nehemiah hoped to be spared was outlined in the prior verses, describing his zeal in following God's laws by honoring the Sabbath.

While Nehemiah desired that God remember deeds of obedience, Nehemiah had already confessed his sins and recognized his failures before God. He knew that it would be through God's love rather than Nehemiah's own achievements that he would be spared, so he made an appeal to God's love and mercy.

Human nature puts forth its best foot first, even in an appeal for mercy. We all seek mercy even while realizing we did not earn any gracious favor. The mindset behind this type of appeal is that, even though we do not earn favor, we possess enough redeeming qualities that perhaps we could be spared. Nehemiah showed his shared humanity with us when making this appeal.

# The Quest for Justice

Nehemiah's third appeal for remembrance comes after dealing with sin in the priestly class: "Remember them, O my God, because they have desecrated the priesthood and the covenant of the priesthood and the Levites" (Neh. 13:29). This appeal is different from the others, because Nehemiah sought for God to remember others rather than himself. But he was not seeking God to remember their good.

Nehemiah dealt with two types of people desecrating the priesthood: those priests who broke the laws, and those who were unqualified yet assumed the role of priest. Both went against God's standard but remained uncorrected until Nehemiah addressed the problems. He fixed the problems, and then asked God to remember their sin.

Is it acceptable to hold others up to God to be remembered for their sin? Isn't that almost like seeking God's favor by pointing out others who we deem are less obedient than we are?

People have expanded and distorted the meaning of "Judge not, that you be not judged" (Matt. 7:1) to imply that we can never comment on anyone else's sin. First, some passages teach against judgment regarding someone's eternal destiny, which is correct. Only God has the authority to make that judgment. But this verse and the following passage refers not to eternal judgment but to evaluating someone else's sin. The warning is that whatever measuring stick we use on someone else will be used on us. It is not a general prohibition against calling out sin, just a reminder that the standard we apply to others will be applied to us.

Still, is it acceptable to call out other people's sins to God as Nehemiah did? We can say that Nehemiah held the same standard for himself as he did for others, so there is no hypocrisy. Also, Nehemiah did not take any action beyond correcting them of their sinful practices. Finally, we see that Nehemiah's focus was on sinful activities going against God's command for spiritual leaders, and not a general campaign against all behavior. He made a focused response against public sinful behavior. We see the same efforts in numerous reform movements throughout church history, seeking to purge corruption and public sin from leaders.

> We can observe and point out sinful behavior, but we must leave the business of judgment to God, for He is both merciful and just.

But that still leaves the unanswered question: is it acceptable to bring this behavior to the attention of God, especially when we know that God already knows everything? What Nehemiah ultimately sought is justice from God. Nehemiah wanted God to evaluate the actions of each individual, particularly those in public service, and compare it to His own standard as written in His Law. We do not know Nehemiah's opinion concerning their eternal destiny. All we see is his opinion concerning their conduct in these matters.

Nehemiah held these actions up for view by God but stopped short of calling for their condemnation. He allowed God to make the final judgment while calling specific activities as sinful. To present these to God is both seeking reassurance that Nehemiah was understanding God's laws properly and seeking God's confirmation regarding right and wrong. Nehemiah understood the actions as wrong based on his reading of God's law. But he wanted justice from God, with part of that justice being an understanding of right and wrong. But Nehemiah left the issue of punishment or mercy in God's hands.

What does a prayer like this accomplish? First, it clarifies God's standards, by confirming what is considered to be sin. Second, it reaffirms that we are walking in obedience to God, at least in this issue, by measuring our lives against the same standard, to ensure that we are not committing the same sin we are denouncing. But finally and most importantly, it is seeking justice from God by not judging others ourselves. We can observe and point out sinful behavior, but we must leave the business of judgment to God, for He is both merciful and just.

## The Quest for God's Companionship

Nehemiah's final prayer for remembrance is the final statement in the book: "Remember me, O my God, for good" (Neh. 13:31). The request is simple. He did not seek remembrance of past deeds or faithfulness, or even the errant ways of others. He just sought God's remembrance "for good." What does this mean?

There are several potential answers, but we will examine two. First, being the last words in Nehemiah's memoirs, he could have been seeking an overall evaluation of his life. We do not know how much longer Nehemiah lived after these events, but his presumed age as a mature adult as cupbearer to the king at the beginning, plus the elapsed time of at least twenty years of events in the book, likely places him at an advanced age by the end here. He may have sought God's endorsement of his life as he attempted to live it out in obedience and service to God. That is the simplest and most straightforward explanation.

But looking at how the book of Nehemiah is structured points to a deeper and more subtle explanation. The book of Nehemiah begins with a report from his brother, which propels Nehemiah into a season of fasting and prayer, culminating in the prayer recorded in the first chapter of the book. The final chapter describes final reforms carried out by Nehemiah, interspersed with prayers of remembrance. The final statement in the book is a prayer.

The book of Nehemiah is bookended by prayer. Prayer is a common thread running through the book. While the beginning prayer follows a more formal style, the shorter prayers are more personal, not even invoking God's name at times, but rather addressing God directly. This saturation of prayer in the book demonstrates that Nehemiah had a personal relationship with God, as seen in a continual prayer life. The final prayer concluding the book can be seen as a request for continued relationship with God.

Did Nehemiah need to beg God for relationship? No, for God desires relationship with us. But since God will allow our sin to sever the closeness of that relationship, Nehemiah was requesting that his efforts at obedience are seen by God as a desire to maintain that relationship. Nehemiah knew that God would not hear the prayers of the sinful and would remove the joy of the relationship, so he wanted to ensure that he was in right relationship and maintaining the strength of the relationship. Nehemiah desired God's companionship.

We can be tempted to rest on our laurels, to feel as if we have done enough for God. I once knew someone whose answers to any request for service was, "I've done that for thirty years—let someone younger do that now." We can believe that enough service has earned us a "lifetime membership," in which no further service is necessary. But Nehemiah understood that God

> We enjoy our relationship with God throughout our lives and into eternity.

does not see it that way. The point of a relationship is continual companionship, not just from past activities, but also present focus and future direction. If we think we have earned God's favor, we have missed the whole point: we cannot earn God's favor, but must receive it as a free gift. Part of that free gift is eternal fellowship with God, which we sustain through obedient walking with God and continual interaction with Him through prayer. This is a relationship that does not have an ending point, but is enjoyed by us with God throughout our lives and into eternity.

# Prayer Building Block #13:
## Continually seek God's companionship.

## How do you view God when you interact with Him?

Are you declaring your accomplishments to Him? Are you comparing yourself favorably with others to Him? Or are you seeking fellowship *with* Him?

Any attempt to curry favor with God through our good deeds will not end well. Once we are in the presence of God and His holiness, all of our efforts will seem meaningless, and we will desire to repent, as did Job, in sackcloth and ashes. Any efforts at making ourselves look better through comparison with the sin of others will also not end well, because God does not grade righteousness on the curve. All efforts at righteousness on our own must either be perfect or face judgment. We cannot earn favor with God on our own merits.

Therefore, we must seek fellowship with God, fellowship available only through His grace and mercy. If you have been following the building blocks through this book, you will find a steady progression from desiring to know God, to removing obstacles that sever fellowship with God, to establishing practices that naturally draw us closer to God. But the underlying question is, why?

## Why do we desire to draw close to God?

To show Him how good we are and the good things we have done on His behalf? To show Him how much better than other people we have been? What is our motivation behind our desire to draw closer to God?

When we read the book of Nehemiah, we see that, as demonstrated by Nehemiah's prayer life, he desired God's companionship. His desire to obey God and serve Him was rooted in love, the love that springs out of a personal relationship. All other reasons will fall short and ultimately fail. No other reason can generate the power and perseverance for lifelong devotion and obedience. Our desire to be close to God should be fueled by a strong drive to be with God.

The first question of the Westminster Shorter Catechism reads: "What is the chief end of man?" The answer? "Man's chief end is to glorify God, and to enjoy him for ever."[3] Notice that last phrase, "*enjoy Him for ever*" (emphasis added). We are to enjoy God, enjoy our fellowship with Him, and that joy will be a springboard for the type of life that will glorify God. Too often we get it backwards by trying to do good things to draw closer to God. We must seek God's presence continually so that, out of our blessed fellowship with God, our love spurs us on to do the sort of things that honor and glorify God. The obedience arises from the relationship.

Seek God's companionship and enjoy His fellowship.

**Rebuilding**

Chapter 14

# The End of the Task is Not the End

*"Now this is not the end. It is not even the beginning of the end.*
*But it is, perhaps, the end of the beginning."*
*— Winston Churchill*[1]

Have you ever watched a movie and felt at the end that it was not really over? Sometimes movies will deliberately position themselves for sequels, leaving many questions wide open. Other movies will painstakingly tie up every loose end. *The Return of the King*, for example, spent what felt like a third of the movie concluding matters and seemed to have three endings. But many movies simply stop rather than come to a conclusion, almost as if they ran out of film before reaching the end of the story.

The book of Nehemiah does not feel that abrupt when it ends. Nehemiah ends his memoirs with a final prayer seeking God's remembrance. However, we are not left with the feeling that a final conclusion has been reached. The initial task, the rebuilding of the Jerusalem wall, came to a fine conclusion at the end of chapter six. But then Nehemiah works on religious reforms, punctuated by a re-reading of the Law and the people rededicating themselves to follow God's law. If the book had ended here, it would have been a fine conclusion.

Except that matters were not concluded. Years passed, sinful practices crept back in, and twenty years later, Nehemiah returned to Jerusalem to straighten out problems. This he did with his characteristic zeal and thoroughness, but we are not left at the end of the book with the sense that all problems have been resolved and will not recur. Sin and problems will return again.

The book of Malachi is chronologically the most recent book in the Old Testament, covering events about thirty-five years after Nehemiah. Malachi dealt with problems among the people and priests similar to what Nehemiah faced. Sometimes the end is not truly the end.

It can be easy to read a book and come to the last page. Novels will conclude and resolve any unanswered questions, except in the case of a book series, in which the reader will be left hanging on several fronts until they purchase the next book. But for non-fiction books, especially those that purport to move the reader to a new place, the end of the book is not the end of the matter. The issue addressed in the book has been influenced but not especially brought to completion.

Such is the case with prayer. These prayer building blocks are designed to guide you toward a deeper relationship with God and a more continual prayer life. But embarking upon them and completing the book does not mean that we have "arrived" at our ideal relationship with God. Transformation, often called sanctification, is a lifelong process, a journey that we take with God for the remainder of our lives. Following these concepts can help propel you onward so that the book does not become just another nice idea placed on a shelf.

## Monuments vs. Milestones

When the Israelites crossed the Jordan River under Joshua, they knew their task had not been completed. Although a few kingdoms east of the river had been defeated, the main job of conquering the Promised Land was just beginning. When they crossed the Jordan River, God had miraculously parted the waters while in flood stage to allow them to cross. God then instructed them to take stones from the river to build a monument on the other side. Except that it wasn't just a monument, it was also a *milestone*.

Monuments are constructed in honor of an individual or group, often in memory of that person or group after they have passed away. Washington, D.C., is filled with monuments to people who are gone, celebrating their accomplishments and contributions to America. But a monument is normally built after the achievements have been finished, when the contribution is complete. There will be no further accomplishments coming from the person or group commemorated by the monument.

Milestones, on the other hand, represent a marker signifying progress. They are statements saying, "We made it this far!" Old roads once had a stone marker at each mile interval, denoting the number of miles to or from a given designation, hence the term "milestone." While there is no guarantee of further progress, the implication is that the job is not yet done, the journey not yet complete. There is more. The milestone stands to denote the progress made to that point, with the goal of continuing on toward a completion.

Milestones can become monuments for future generations, to remember what had been done in the past. That was how God intended the stones from the Jordan River to be used. They were to be a sign for the future, when people might not personally remember God's mighty act of parting the river so that Israel could cross safely. The stones were a memorial to remember that God had worked for them in the past, and would continue to work for them in the present and future.

> **The milestone stands to denote the progress made to that point, with the goal of continuing on toward a completion.**

But for the present generation, the one that collected the stones and built the monument, the stones were a milestone. God had brought Israel to this point, just as He promised. This marker was a message that God was in the process of fulfilling His promises, and would not stop until His promises were completely fulfilled.

We need to adopt the same attitude in our lives, by establishing milestones of significant events in our lives. The inside of my wedding band has a note to my wife. Every time I remember that note, I remember the pledge I made to my bride on our wedding day. Although physical markers help, milestones can also be spiritual. We can mentally drive a stake in the ground or build a pile of stones in our hearts to declare, "God was with me to this point!" That declaration becomes a reminder of God's promise to continue with us to the end.

# Shelf vs. Life

A big concern in the business world is that training will not result in lasting change. People will enjoy a class, appreciate the material, and agree that the new concepts are beneficial. But when they return to their offices, the binder with the good concepts and valuable information goes on a shelf to gather dust. Minds were enlightened but there was no lasting change.

The same problem can occur with church retreats. People set aside their lives for a weekend and encounter God in a focused and powerful way, not distracted by the busyness of life. Tears are shed, confessions made, and desires to more completely surrender to God are expressed. Then they come home from the retreat, reenter their busy lives, and the sheen of the retreat slowly wears off. They return to their former state, and there is no lasting transformation.

Peter had the first "mountaintop" experience, when he experienced Jesus in His glory. Peter makes a powerful declaration of Jesus as the Messiah. Then, in the next chapter, down off the mountain, Peter then makes a statement so foolish that Jesus rebukes him, equating him with Satan. How do we turn these mountaintop experiences into lasting transformations?

We must *live* the change. Any new information not put into practice is forgotten or rendered irrelevant. It is not only our minds that must change, but our whole person. It is the Spirit within us that works God's transforming power. We use our minds to take in new concepts and learn new ideas, acquiring information to be more effective. But it is God's Spirit that works in our hearts any lasting change. We start by living out the concepts. Then God starts the transformation work.

# Rest vs. Catching Your Breath

When we have reached a certain milestone, it can be tempting to declare the task done and rest. The job may not be completely done, but if it is mostly done, we allow ourselves to stop. Many home repair projects end in this fashion. Once something is in place and functional, it can be easy to stop, especially if other projects are clamoring for attention. So it doesn't get painted or caulked, or the finishing touches to make it nice get set aside. Permanently.

What may be acceptable in our homes does not work in God's kingdom. Because of the human proclivity toward sin, continual effort must be made to resist sin and conform to God. Any periods of rest will cause us to atrophy spiritually. The first astronauts in space for more than a few hours experienced severe muscle atrophy. NASA did not realize how powerfully our muscles were working every moment to resist gravitational forces, even just by the effort of standing and walking. Once in space, the forces of gravity were so slight, muscles immediately went into

> It is God's Spirit that works in our hearts any lasting change.

atrophy, and sometimes astronauts needed to be lifted out of the spaceship after returning to earth. Later flights built in strenuous exercise regimes to counter the naturally occurring muscle loss.

We combat similar forces of spiritual atrophy when we rest. We need to recognize that we must keep pursuing God to counter the natural forces that pull us away from Him. We need to adopt a new mindset that considers rest to be our eternal state of security and peace in Christ. As for this world, we should never consider our task done.

We may get tired and need times of Sabbath. These even may be periods of seeming restfulness. But we must never consider ourselves in permanent rest in this world. We must consider these times of Sabbath as "catching our breath." Just as an athlete in training may pause to catch their breath, after which they then resume their activity, we will have times when we need to catch our breath, and then, refreshed, resume our life calling of following and serving Christ.

It may not look dramatically different from your life today. But the attitude will change your heart, and you will approach life as a series of adventures with God, rather than a set of tasks after which you can retire and enter permanent rest.

## The Finish Line

When Nehemiah completed his memoirs with his closing prayer for remembrance, it did not mean that he was finished. He had completed his current tasks, but the text does not say or even suggest that he was done. Nehemiah likely returned to his job as cupbearer to the king, keeping tabs on the Jerusalem community to ensure they did not deviate from God's commands. He did not retire from serving God or praying to God. Nehemiah's finish line was the end of his life.

Each one of us has to decide whether we want to walk with God all our days or depart from God after a season. The Bible recounts many who abandoned God later in life, including Solomon, who was drawn away from God by his numerous wives, and King Saul, who created great misery for others through his rebellion against God.

Do we truly love God? If we do, each day will be a joy, delighting in God's presence even when circumstances are less favorable. Our lives will feel like an adventure of walking with God, trusting Him while eagerly anticipating what happens next in our lives.

If we do not love God, but are instead obeying God through a sense of duty, the very thought of having to stick with God all our days will fill us with dread. Instead of an adventure, it will feel more like a death march, shackled to our duty until we fall in the dust. Life will be bleak and wrought with responsibilities and burdens, which we will piously declare to others are our "crosses to bear."

> We practice that fellowship through a lifestyle of prayer, in which communication with God is as natural and continual as breathing.

Which life sounds more like the abundant life promised by Jesus? Which life realizes the joy promised by God? Which life better reflects the salvation of God to a lost and dying world?

We can love God and walk in fellowship with Him, serving Him out of the overflow of love that He pours into us, or we can grit our teeth and resolve to do our best for God out of duty. The latter was practiced by those who elevated the law, using it to control lives in the hope they would be acceptable to God. But the former is the promise given to us by Jesus, who promised to never leave or forsake us. He desires to be in fellowship with us. We experience that fellowship through the Holy Spirit. We practice that fellowship through a lifestyle of prayer, in which communication with God is as natural and continual as breathing.

# Prayer Building Block #14:
## Build your relationship with God forever.

Lather. Rinse. Repeat. My friend James Watkins makes light of these simple instructions, afraid that we will be caught in an endless hair washing cycle if we follow the directions precisely, because the last instruction is "repeat." Shampoo users know to only repeat the process once. But should we stop the cycle in our spiritual lives?

Do we ever reach a point where we ever stop praying and seeking God? Do we ever attain a position where we never need to work on an attitude of surrender to God? Do we ever arrive at a place where we are "close enough to God" and don't need to work on our relationship with God anymore? The answer to these questions is: *no*.

If we love God, the efforts to draw closer to Him and walk in fellowship with Him should not be perceived as work. It should be a joy, deeper and more sublime than anything we experience on earth. It will take effort on our part, but it should be a labor of love, pursuing the God who first loved us.

But sadly, because of our sin nature, forces within us will keep resisting the call of God. We will want our own way rather than submitting to God. The lures of the world will continue their siren calls, seeking to draw us away from God and even deceive us into believing our sin is somehow serving God. As Paul so explicitly describes the war raging within us:

"So I find it to be a law that when I want to do right, evil lies close at hand. For I delight in the law of God, in my inner being, but I see in my members another law waging war against the law of my mind and making me captive to the law of sin that dwells in my members" (Rom. 7:21–23).

We cannot condemn ourselves due to this reality, because it is the sin nature in ongoing rebellion against God. But we also cannot use this war and sin nature as an excuse to continue in sin. God has won the victory over sin; we just have to claim the victory in the specific areas of our lives in which we struggle.

## Rebuilding

So we will struggle, but we will not be alone in our struggles. We have God's indwelling Spirit ready to guide, lead, and instruct us. We have God ready to transform us by the renewing of our minds. We have Christ as our advocate and friend, ready to walk beside us and plead our case. Unless it is our choice, we will never be alone for the remainder of our lives.

Pursue God and walk with God today. Repeat. Forever.

# Notes

## Introduction

1    *The Holy Bible, English Standard Version,* (Wheaton, IL: Crossway, a publishing ministry of Good News Publishers, 2001), Nehemiah 1:1.

2    Rainer Albertz, *A History of Israelite Religion in the Old Testament Period* (trans. Bowden, John; 2 vols.; Louisville, KY: Westminster John Knox Press, 1994), 1:198.

## Chapter 1

1    *Apollo 13*, directed by Ron Howard (1995; Universal City, CA: Universal Studios, 1995), VHS.

2    Gordon Franz, Notes from Lectures during Class Trip to Israel (Through Lancaster Bible College, 2007), 6/30, Lachish.

## Chapter 2

1    Homer, *The Odyssey* (trans. Rouse, W. H. D. Rouse, New York: Mentor Books, 1949), 114.

2    Rainer Albertz, *A History of Israelite Religion in the Old Testament Period* (trans. Bowden, John; 2 vols.; Louisville, KY: Westminster John Knox Press, 1994), 1:37, 100.

3    Helmer Ringgren, *Israelite Religion* (trans. Green, David E.; Philadelphia, PA: Fortress Press, 1963), 45, 95–98, 267.

4    Rainer Albertz, *Israel in Exile: The History and Literature of the Sixth Century B.C.E.* (Atlanta, GA: Society of Biblical Literature, 2001), 106–109.

## Chapter 3

1      Joshua Spodek, "2 Endearing Vince Lombardi Quotes Reveal the Source of His Leadership" Inc.com, (June 10, 2016).

## Chapter 4

1      Ernest Hemingway, "A Clean, Well-Lighted Place," *Scribner's Magazine* 93, no. 3, (1933), 149–150.

2      *Signs*, directed by M. Night Shyamalan (2002; Burbank, CA: Touchstone Pictures, 2003), DVD.

## Chapter 5

1      Walt Kelly, *We Have Met the Enemy, and He is Us* (New York, NY: Simon & Schuster, 1987).

2      Jim Collins, *Good to Great* (New York, NY: Harper Collins, 2001), 178–180.

## Chapter 6

1      Bill Watterson. *Scientific Progress Goes "Boink": A Calvin & Hobbes Collection* (Kansas City, MO: Andrews McMeel Publishing, 1991), 101.

## Chapter 7

1      Leonard Roy Frank, ed., *Quotationary*, (New York: Random House, 2001), 835.

2      Jackson Seynonga, *PrayerQuake Conference* (Phoenix, AZ: BridgeBuilders, 2004), Conference Speaker 06/09/2004.

3      Ibid.

## Chapter 8

1      Brother Lawrence, *The Practice of the Presence of God* (Peabody, MA: Hendrickson, 2003), 42.

2      Ibid, 4.

3      Ibid, 9.

4      Ibid, 18.

5      Ibid, 26.

6        Ibid, 48.

## Chapter 9

1        Henry Mintzburg, *The Rise and Fall of Strategic Planning* (New York, NY: Simon & Schuster, 1994), 412.
2        Jim Collins, *Good to Great* (New York: Harper Collins, 2001), 178–180.
3        Joseph Blenkinsopp, *Ezra—Nehemiah: A Commentary* (Philadelphia, PA: Westminster Press, 1988), 248.
4        F. Charles Fensham, *The Books of Ezra and Nehemiah* (Grand Rapids, MI: Eerdmans, 1982), 184.

## Chapter 10

1        *The Holy Bible, English Standard Version,* (Wheaton, IL: Crossway, a publishing ministry of Good News Publishers, 2001), Ezekiel 25:17.

## Chapter 11

1        Bill Watterson, *Attack of the Deranged Mutant Killer Monster Snowgoons: A Calvin & Hobbes Collection* (Kansas City, MO: Andrews McMeel Publishing, 1992), 62.
2        *Archaeological Study Bible, New International Version*, (Grand Rapids, MI: Zondervan, 2005), 697.
3        D.A. Baer & R.P. Gordon, *NIDOTTE* (ed. Van Gemeren, Willem A.; vol. 2; Grand Rapids, MI: Zondervan), 64, 71.
         Derek Kidner, *Ezra and Nehemiah: An Introduction and Commentary* (vol. 11; Downers Grove, IL: InterVarsity Press, 1979), 99.
         Jacob M. Myers, *Ezra-Nehemiah* (New York, NY: Doubleday, 1965), 136.

## Chapter 12

1        Philip Dormer Stanhope, 4th Earl Chesterfield, *Lord Chesterfield, Letters Written to His Son On the Fine Art of Becoming a Man of the World and a Gentleman, 1750* (www.gutenberg.net: Project Gutenberg, 2004), 18.

2     Charles R. Swindoll, *Growing Wise in Family Life* (Portland, OR: Multnomah Press, 1988), 89–94.

## Chapter 13
1     James Dobson, Speech given at Liberty University, September 26, 2016.
2     Ben Olan, *Big Time Baseball* (New York, NY: Hart Publishing, 1965), 30.
3     Anonymous, *Westminster Shorter Catechism* (London: The Big Nest (Christian Classics), 2016), 5.

## Chapter 14
1     Leonard Roy Frank, ed., *Quotationary*, (New York: Random House, 2001), 58.

# Scripture Index

# Rebuilding

# Bibliography

Albertz, Rainer, *A History of Israelite Religion in the Old Testament Period* (trans. Bowden, John; 2 vols.; Louisville, KY: Westminster John Knox Press, 1994), Vol. 1.

Anonymous, *Westminster Shorter Catechism* (London: The Big Nest (Christian Classics), 2016).

*Archaeological Study Bible, New International Version*, (Grand Rapids, MI: Zondervan, 2005).

Baer, D.A., & Gordon, R.P., *NIDOTTE* (ed. Van Gemeren, Willem A.; vol. 2; Grand Rapids, MI: Zondervan).

Blenkinsopp, Joseph, *Ezra-Nehemiah: A Commentary* (Philadelphia, PA: Westminster Press, 1988).

Dobson, James, Speech given at Liberty University, September 26, 2016.

Fensham, F. Charles, *The Books of Ezra and Nehemiah* (Grand Rapids, MI: Eerdmans, 1982).

Frank, Leonard Roy, ed., *Quotationary*, (New York: Random House, 2001).

Franz, Gordon, Notes from Lectures during Class Trip to Israel (Through Lancaster Bible College, 2007), 6/30, Lachish.

Hemingway, Ernest, "A Clean, Well-Lighted Place," *Scribner's Magazine* 93, no. 3, (1933).

Homer, *The Odyssey* (trans. Rouse, W. H. D. Rouse, New York: Mentor Books, 1949).

Howard, Ron, dir., *Apollo 13* (1995; Universal City, CA: Universal Studios, 1995), VHS.

Kelly, Walt, *We Have Met the Enemy and He is Us* (New York, NY: Simon & Schuster, 1987).

Kidner, Derek, *Ezra and Nehemiah: An Introduction and Commentary* (vol. 11; Downers Grove, IL: InterVarsity Press, 1979).

Lawrence, Brother, *The Practice of the Presence of God* (Peabody, MA: Hendrickson, 2003).

Mintzburg, Henry, *The Rise and Fall of Strategic Planning* (New York, NY: Simon & Schuster, 1994).

Myers, Jacob M., *Ezra—Nehemiah* (New York, NY: Doubleday, 1965).

*The Holy Bible, English Standard Version,* (Wheaton, IL: Crossway, a publishing ministry of Good News Publishers, 2001).

Olan, Ben, *Big Time Baseball* (New York, NY: Hart Publishing, 1965).

Ringgren, Helmer, *Israelite Religion* (trans. Green, David E.; Philadelphia, PA: Fortress Press, 1963).

Seynonga, Jackson, *PrayerQuake Conference* (Phoenix, AZ: BridgeBuilders, 2004), Conference Speaker 06/09/2004.

Shyamalan, M. Night, dir. *Signs*, 2002; Burbank, CA: Touchstone Pictures, 2003, DVD.

Spodek, Joshua, "2 Endearing Vince Lombardi Quotes Reveal the Source of His Leadership" Inc.com, (June 10, 2016).

Stanhope, Philip Dormer, 4th Earl Chesterfield, *Lord Chesterfield, Letters Written to His Son On the Fine Art of Becoming a Man of the World and a Gentleman, 1750* (www.gutenberg.net: Project Gutenberg, 2004).

Swindoll, Charles R., *Growing Wise in Family Life* (Portland, OR: Multnomah Press, 1988).

Watterson, Bill, *Attack of the Deranged Mutant Killer Monster Snowgoons: A Calvin & Hobbes Collection* (Kansas City, MO: Andrews McMeel Publishing, 1992).

Watterson, Bill, *Scientific Progress Goes "Boink": A Calvin & Hobbes Collection* (Kansas City, MO: Andrews McMeel Publishing, 1991).

Made in the USA
Lexington, KY
06 May 2019